UNIVE... ...INGHAM

WITHDRAWN

ROM THE LIBRARY

D0192748

OUR NATIONAL LIFE

Our
National Life

EDITED BY
ALLISTER VALE

*Published to celebrate the
150th Anniversary
of The National Club*

NOTTINGHAM UNIVERSITY LIBRARY

THE NATIONAL CLUB
LONDON

with

MONARCH BOOKS
Mill Hill, London

Copyright © The National Club 1998

First published by Monarch Books 1998.

ISBN 1 85424 391 8

All rights reserved.
No part of this publication may be reproduced or
transmitted in any form or by any means, electronic
or mechanical, including photocopy, recording or any
information storage and retrieval system, without
permission in writing from Monarch Books
in association with Angus Hudson Ltd,
Concorde House, Grenville Place,
Mill Hill London, NW7 3SA.

Editorial Office: Monarch Books,
Broadway House, The Broadway, Crowborough,
East Sussex TN6 1HQ.

British Library Cataloguing Data
A catalogue record for this book is available
from the British Library.

1001638645

Enquiries about The National Club should
be directed to:
The National Club
c/o 69 St James Street
London SW1A 1PJ

Designed and produced for the Publishers by
Bookprint Creative Services
P.O. Box 827, BN21 3YJ, England.
Printed in Great Britain.

CONTENTS

FOREWORD

It is appropriate that to mark its 150th year The National Club should issue a book dealing with the application of the original principles of its foundation to our situation today.

There is no doubt that a great deal has changed since 1845 in the circumstances in which we live. However, human nature in its essential characteristics of seeking to be motivated by a purpose in life and of seeking to achieve satisfaction in the degree to which that purpose is attained, remains now as it was then.

I found the contributions to this anniversary book to be both thought provoking and challenging. Written from the standpoint of the Protestant Christian they cover a great variety of the areas of life which pose formidable problems today. From the old problem of the framework which should determine conduct in the market-place, through the part that education has to play in our modern life, to the new problems posed for us by developments in genetics and the development of substances with dangerous and yet to some attractive qualities, experts in their fields show how the illumination of Christianity applies to the way forward. An important message of these papers is that Christians have no right to inflict their values on others but they do have a right in a free democracy to proclaim the values they hold dear as forcefully and attractively as possible.

I would sum up the lesson of these papers in the conclusion of the paper on genetic manipulation: 'We need a spirit of wisdom to enable us to exercise responsible stewardship in an attitude of dependence on God so that the benefits are harnessed while the weak, the vulnerable and the environment are protected.'

Although said particularly in relationship to the technology of genetic manipulation—which is described as an immensely powerful God-given tool which we can use for the relief of suffering and to help overcome some of the problems that beset our overcrowded world—I think this final lesson is of general application to all the other subject matters dealt with in the book.

Mackay of Clashfern

PREFACE

What is the best way to celebrate a 150th anniversary?

The choice appeared to be between an indulgent look backwards or an attempt to look forwards. The Club records indicate that the 100th anniversary, coinciding with the end of the Second World War, was a rather muted occasion. The temptation to make good the lacklustre 1945 celebration with a more elaborate backward look was therefore strong. In the end it was resisted in favour of a clear statement of what The National Club wanted to see on the nation's agenda for the future.

This book is that agenda.

Not all the issues that concern the Club have been addressed, such as abortion or crime and punishment. However, the issues covered are areas of concern to all members of the United Kingdom. The contributions are written by acknowledged experts in the fields addressed. That each author writes from an unashamedly and distinctly Christian perspective is the unique contribution of the book to the issues under debate.

The National Club has always been concerned with moral issues from a biblical perspective. Indeed, two of its 'general objectives' were to 'maintain the Protestant principles of the constitution in the administration of public affairs' and 'to uphold a system of National Education based on Scripture . . .'. While some of the issues that gave rise to the Club's formation in June 1845 have passed into history, the Club has always sought to test issues and policies by the yardstick of Scripture. That is still the case today.

The National Club does not claim to have all the answers. But it does want to bring to the attention of the Nation the principles that are to be found in the Bible. These principles will act as a rudder in the amoral and pragmatic seas in which we now find ourselves afloat.

I wish to thank the authors for their efforts and patience. The views they express are not necessarily those of The National Club, but all write from a Christian perspective. In particular I wish to acknowledge Dr Allister Vale's contribution as honorary editor. He has spent unnumbered hours in bringing this book to fruition.

Andrew Symonds

CONTRIBUTORS

James Allcock OBE
Formerly, Director of Gas Supplies, British Gas plc

Alasdair Barron MSc
Lately, Director of Credit Action; e-business Communications, IBM(UK)

The Revd Dr Roger Beckwith MA BD DD
Honorary Librarian, Latimer House, Oxford

Dr Caroline Berry MB PhD FRCP
Lately, Consultant Clinical Geneticist, Guy's Hospital, London

Professor Robert Berry MA PhD DSc FRSE
Professor of Genetics, University College London

Dr David Cook MA PhD
Director, Whitefield Institute; Fellow and Chaplain of Green College, Oxford

Sir Timothy Hoare Bt OBE MA
Chairman, The National Club; Member of the General Synod of the Church of England; Member of the Chadwick Commission on Church and State

The Rt Hon the Lord Mackay of Clashfern KT PC LLD FRSE Hon FRCPE Hon FRCSE Hon FRCOG
The Lord Chancellor, 1987–97

Professor the Lord McColl of Dulwich CBE MS FRCS FRCSE FACS
Professor of Surgery, United Medical and Dental Schools of Guy's and St Thomas's Hospitals, London; Parliamentary Private Secretary to the Prime Minister, 1994–97; Vice-President, The National Club.

Andrew Symonds FRICS ACI Arb
Chairman, The National Club, 1989–1996

The Rt Revd John Taylor KCVO MA LLD (Hon)
President, The National Club; Formerly, Bishop of St Albans

Keith Tondeur JP
Director, Credit Action

Dr John Tripp MD FRCP FRCPCH
Senior Lecturer in Child Health, Postgraduate Medical School, University of Exeter; Consultant Paediatrician, Royal Devon and Exeter Hospital, Exeter.

Dr Robert Twycross DM FRCP FRCR
Macmillan Clinical Reader in Palliative Medicine, University of Oxford

Dr Allister Vale MD FRCP FRCPE FRCPG FFOM
Director, National Poisons Information Service (Birmingham Centre), West Midlands Poisons Unit, City Hospital, Birmingham

Professor Duncan Vere MD FRCP FFPM
Emeritus Professor of Therapeutics, University of London; Consulting Physician, Royal London Hospital, London

Richard Wilkins BD
General Secretary, Association of Christian Teachers, St Albans

Claire Wilson-Thomas BSc
Public Policy Department, Christian Action, Research and Education (CARE), London

CHAPTER ONE

WHAT MAKES A NATION GREAT?

Timothy Hoare

Sir Timothy Hoare has been a member of the General Synod of the Church of England since 1970 and was a member of the Chadwick Commission on Church and State. He became Chairman of The National Club in 1997.

One of the best known definitions of a nation came, rather surprisingly, from Joseph Stalin, 'A nation is a historically evolved, state community of language, territory, economic life and psychological make-up, manifested in a community of culture.'[1] The biblical record of humanity's beginnings describes, but more gracefully, almost identical elements in distinguishing one nation from another. (These two authorities share less agreement about what constitutes national greatness and about how it may be achieved!)

National identity

When The National Club was founded in 1845, Great Britain had been a single nation for little more than a century. Yet it was close to the apogee of its imperial power. It has been called 'an invented nation' and even now many of our fellow citizens think of themselves first as Welsh or West Indian.

Linda Colley has argued that because it lacked historical coherence, a strong sense of national identity was fundamental to the creation of the British nation, let alone its advance to any degree of greatness. She describes the other characteristics which influenced the 'forging of Britain': geography, a common language, racial qualities (such as tenacity and independence) and success in trade and war. But the most powerful contribution to our national identity was made, in her judgement, by Protestantism. 'Protestantism was the foundation which made the invention of Great Britain possible.'[2]

A nation under God?

It had been their religion which had originally given the English that sense of being special, of being set apart by God. This was not an experience unique to the English but it was very real and it provided a strong sense of purpose in national life. In 1537 Bishop Hugh Latimer wrote of the long-awaited birth of Prince Edward, 'Verily God hath showed Himself God of England or rather, an English God.'[3] A century later Milton echoed the claim, 'God is decreeing to begin some new and great period . . . What does He then but reveal Himself to His servants, and as His manner is, first to His Englishmen . . . though we mark not the method of His counsels and are unworthy.'[4]

To us these may seem quaint and even arrogant assertions of national pride but they expressed that sense of national calling and purpose which arguably underlay much of the later colonial, military and missionary expansion which became the British Empire. In a similar way, in the Old Testament, Israel's leaders claimed to be God's instruments. It is a striking feature of their history that whenever national greatness was promised to, or claimed by the Israelites, it was not expressed in purely selfish or narrowly nationalistic terms. Other nations would benefit from Israel's greatness. Psalm 67 (which the *Book of Common Prayer* appropriately sets for the marriage service, another relationship which should carry God's grace to others) affirms this ideal, 'God be gracious to us and bless us . . . that His ways may be known on earth and His saving power among all the nations.'[5]

Truly great nations, in their noblest moments, have held to a vision that their influence will help, rather than exploit, others. At times in the history of our nation that sense of being used to help others has been evident. The decorative paintings by William Dyce (c.1850) in the Royal Robing Room in Parliament, which describe some of the virtues of a Christian ruler (courtesy, generosity, hospitality, mercy, etc.) were more than a fantasy. They were to be seen as illustrating the ideal of how the Sovereign in Parliament should rule the British Empire.

Crisis of national identity?

Today some of the forces that created Great Britain appear to be in decline. As Lord Beloff and others have argued, the nation faces a new identity crisis as a result, for example, of its development towards a multicultural society[6]. Britain is not alone in facing a crisis of identity because the revolution in communication has shrunk the world, challenging the independence and integrity of nations which are being drawn into larger cultural and economic groups. Indeed it seems that the very concept of nationhood is under threat. It is timely to consider why nations exist and whether they will serve any useful purpose in the next century.

True patriotism

From Horace's 'Dulce et decorum est pro patria mori'[7] to Walter Scott's romantic vision of Robert the Bruce: 'His was the Patriot's burning thought, Of freedom's battle bravely fought',[8] love of one's country was for several centuries enshrined as one of the highest ideals. Patriotism in Britain is now often subjugated to the more politically correct doctrine of solidarity with the common humanity of all. Indeed nationalism, degraded to racial hatred or to envy of another's territory, is blamed for many of the miseries of the twentieth century, as it was in Wilfred Owen's poem 'Dulce et Decorum est', which he called 'the old lie'.[9]

But patriotism remains an honourable value which springs from the same source as love for one's neighbour. As De Tocqueville remarked, 'Few will burn with ardent love for the entire human species. The interests of the human race are better served by giving every man a particular fatherland than by trying to inflame his passions for the whole human race.'[10] For nations, like families, exist primarily for the benefit of their people and national greatness has generally been measured by a nation's degree of self-determination, its influence and its wealth. It is assumed that if a nation possesses these things its people will be contented, but history suggests true national greatness requires more than freedom and prosperity.

True national greatness

One of the most striking examples of individual leadership, leading to national greatness, can be found in the Old Testament account of Moses as, under God, he turned a rabble of slaves into a nation whose influence and power were to peak in the time of King Solomon. At the very outset of his leadership, when his people were newly liberated, Moses recorded the terms on which their future greatness was to be built. Their obedience to God's laws, summarised in the Ten Commandments, will 'show your wisdom and understanding to the nations, who will hear about all these decrees and say, "Surely this great nation is a

16

wise and understanding people.'"[11] The characteristic, above all others, which marked out the Israelite nation in their times of greatness, was obedience to God's law. That also had been the condition attached to the promise of national greatness which God made to their ancestor Abraham. God's promise of national greatness to both Abraham and Moses was dependent not on the quality of their leadership but on the obedience of their people, for which the leader held some responsibility.

Obedience to the divine moral code

Ever since then, the idea that national greatness is linked to obedience to the divine moral code has undergirded Judaeo-Christian civilisation and is mirrored in the Muslim world, although with fundamentally different intentions and results. We read in the Old Testament how the fortunes of the Israelites rose and fell according to the attention they gave to the laws of God and the warnings of his prophets. The idea is put pithily in the Book of Proverbs: 'Righteousness exalts a nation.'[12] In Proverbs we also read that stability in a nation has the same source: '[A] throne is established through righteousness.'[13] The example of Moses, as this proverb implies, suggests that national leaders have some responsibility for public morality. It is encouraging that the present Government has expressed its determination to allow moral concerns to influence its policies. Righteousness should be their goal as much as material welfare or 'punching heavier than our weight' in international affairs.

Richard Hooker, the Anglican divine, expressed this duty of rulers in colourful terms: 'A gross error it is to think that regal power ought to serve for man's temporal peace, and not for their eternal safety; as if God had ordained kings for no other end and purpose but only to fat up men like hogs, and to see that they have their mast [food].'[14] Hooker wrote, at the time of the Tudor religious settlement, to defend the royal supremacy in the church.

Monarch, church and state

The Anglican reformers developed the theory of the godly prince, through which they likened the English monarchs to the kings of Israel and expected them to take responsibility for the church and the moral condition of the nation. The monarch, closely bound to the Church of England, by the coronation oath, to preserve its established status and, consecrated to God by anointing, has been endowed with an almost mystical aura, as governor of the church as well as the state. This has enhanced the authority of the crown and reinforced its power as a symbol of national identity and unity. The theory of the godly prince has served as the bedrock of the relationship of church and state, reminding the ruling power that it is answerable to God for its stewardship. 'We have consecrated our civil government by allying it with religion.'[15]

In practice, since Tudor times, the sovereign has only rarely given a strong Christian lead to the nation. Without being sycophantic, it seems a reasonable judgement that, in the light of history, we have been singularly blessed in this respect in the last six decades. The Christmas broadcasts by the Queen and her father and his wartime speeches and national calls to prayer have been exceptional examples of Christian leadership from the throne.

In a democracy, in particular, a nation's leaders cannot successfully sustain public morals by their own example or fiat. Of equal or greater significance are the underlying moral and religious attitudes and affiliations of their people. The Anglican reformers argued that the close identity of the members of the church and the people of England justified government of the church through the crown in Parliament. As recently as the turn of this century, the then Bishop of

London was able to say, 'I am not ashamed to own that I am an Englishman first and a Churchman afterwards. But to my mind Church and State are not contradictory things but the nation looked at from different points of view.'[16]

That was an ideal which contained much reality in Tudor times but by the end of the nineteenth century, as a result of the strength of nonconformity, the growth of rational humanism, and the weakness of the Church of England in many urban areas, there were many English people who would have denied affiliation to the Church of England. The identity of church and nation was becoming more difficult to argue. Since then, to the Christian eye the picture has grown darker, with an apparent steady decline in churchgoing and in private and public morality. As even Moses found, however strong the leadership and however committed it may be to maintaining obedience to the divine law, it can be outweighed by the attitudes and standards of ordinary people.

Since the conversion of the Roman Emperor Constantine, all nations which have made some public affirmation of the Christian faith have been conscious that its reality in national life has to be measured in practice by the conformity of the civil laws (as closely as possible) to the divine moral law. Christians, who read about the lessons which the Israelites had learnt the hard way, have been concerned to prevent their nations from making the same mistakes.

Milton in *Paradise Regained* pointed his readers to the prophets:

> In them is plainest taught and easiest learnt
> What makes a nation happy, and keeps it so,
> What ruins kingdoms, and lays cities flat.[17]

The context in the poem is that Satan is tempting Christ with an alternative to obedience to God's word; the model of the power of Rome—greatness through might. Rome was indeed by most measures a great nation. To her citizens 'she was the eternal city which had given them peace, the fount of law, the centre of civilisation, the Mecca of poets and orators and artists but also a home of every kind of idolatrous worship'.[18] And Rome fell.

One of history's ironies is that the sack of Rome occurred so soon after the conversion of the Emperor to Christianity. The Church had come to believe that with a Christian emperor, the arrival of the kingdom of God was imminent and it was shaken when pagans blamed Rome's defeat on the rejection of the old gods. Augustine's *City of God* was written partly to address this crisis. Like Paul, Augustine reminds Christians that God stands above all earthly rulers and that 'Christians are the salvation of the commonwealth for they fulfil the highest role of citizenship because they obey the King who stands above all secular rulers'.[19] The *City of God* has had a profound influence on the last 1,500 years of Western Christendom.

The understanding that to God alone properly belongs absolute authority has underpinned the rule of law and the separation of powers (the division of the ruling authority into legislature, judiciary and the executive) in the constitutions of many nations. 'Christianity was the most important force in shaping the constitutions of the states of Europe.'[20]

Christian ideals in national life

If Christians are to be 'the salvation' of their country and promote its greatness, what can be done? Now at the end of the millennium, when the Christian ideals of national life appear to be threatened, we may usefully turn again to Augustine who wrote for a world which also appeared to be falling apart. Today, as then, trusted institutions seem to be failing, old values are being forgotten and our rulers often cease to deserve respect. Augustine's purpose was to help Christians handle their dual citizenship in such circumstances. (Although he was in truth only applying Scripture: 'For here we do not have an enduring city, but we are looking for the city that is to come.')[21]

Christians must obey their rulers and seek the good of the society in which God has set them, while keeping their eyes towards the 'City of God'. His teaching remains a powerful corrective to those who think they can build God's kingdom on earth, an objective which is always frustrated by human frailty and sin. Yet he warns Christians not to opt out of their responsibility to ensure that God's laws are applied to every aspect of national life.

A modern theologian, Lesslie Newbigin, expresses the same challenge: 'A preaching of the Gospel that calls men and women to accept Jesus as Saviour but does not make it clear that discipleship means commitment to a vision of society radically different from that which controls our public life today must be condemned as false.'[22] Christians should be an unsettling, even subversive, force in politics. Christian hope can be creative in motivating reform but it deprives the Christian from ever bestowing total loyalty to a constitution, programme, party or even to one's country.

Yet it is my conviction that paradoxically the potential greatness of any nation can be unlocked by this same Christian hope which has in the past proved such a powerful dynamic for change and yet an anchor of stability. Many, for example Hookyas, have argued that the discoveries of science and the enterprise that led to the industrial revolution depended on the transformation of Christendom's intellectual life by the forces of the Reformation.[23]

Similarly, Christians had a substantial impact on the social life of Great Britain when they took the divine law seriously. William Wilberforce wrote in 1797 when our Christian democracy, such as it then was, was threatened in Britain by the forces unleashed by the French Revolution: 'My only solid hopes for the well being of my country depend not so much on her fleets and armies, not so much on the wisdom of her rulers, or the spirit of her people, as on the persuasion that she still contains many, who, in a degenerate age, love and obey the Gospel of Christ.'[24]

Central to many of the advances in science and their practical application, as well as in the courage of those who stood against the immorality of their contemporaries, was the certainty (a word interchangeable with hope in the Christian vocabulary) that God would honour those who obeyed him and took his word as their guide. Wilberforce was not disappointed, but history tends to be cyclical. Christians face a similar challenge today. The future of our nation rests now to a significant extent in the hands of Christians.

Lessons of history

We are right to be proud of the achievements of liberal democracy, but the collapse of communism, at least in Europe, its most recent alternative ideology, must not tempt us to believe the view of the American philosopher Francis Fukuyama that history having come to an end, our freedoms are secure. Herbert Butterfield, writing in the aftermath of the defeat of the Nazi regime which threatened the existence of democracy in our continent only fifty years ago, reminded us that 'the river of time is littered with the ruins of systems of government which looked perfect in their day'.[25] Like many historians, Butterfield thought he could perceive the operation of moral judgements in history; for example, the debasing of idealistic revolutions which discarded the moral law and degenerated into dictatorships. Butterfield saw the decline of a nation or civilisation as an inevitable result of disobedience to the moral law, although such an outcome might be a long time in coming. He concludes his book with the reflection that essential as is the role of national leaders, 'It is impossible to measure the vast difference that ordinary Christian piety has made to the last two thousand years of European history; but we shall have some inkling of that difference if the world continues on its present drift towards paganism.'[25] That, perhaps, is the key contribution which all Christians have to make to the life of their nations.

Butterfield wrote fifty years ago and our nation seems now to have travelled further down the road towards paganism and its accompanying self-indulgence. Today we may have a better understanding of the seriousness of his warning. We can learn also from our history by looking back to the social condition of Britain in the latter half of the eighteenth century and we may take encouragement from the moral revolution that occurred during the first half of the nineteenth century. The sociologist Christie Davies describes that change, 'It was a period of striking moral reform in personal behaviour which transformed Britain from being a violent, dishonest and addicted society into a peaceable, law-abiding, respectable and essentially moral realm.'[26] It is well illustrated by the story which Walter Scott told of his kinswoman. In old age she blushed when she glanced at novels which she recalled reading aloud to mixed company in her youth. Moral change in society remains a possibility.

Righteousness exalts a nation

The moral influence of Christians in society has generally been welcomed by those of other faiths or none, even if Christians sometimes justify the accusation of being hypocrites. But Butterfield's point about the value to society of the practice of Christian morality needs to be balanced by some words of his contemporary, T.S. Eliot: 'To justify Christianity because it provides a foundation of morality, instead of showing the necessity of Christian morality from the truth of Christianity is a very dangerous inversion.'[27]

It is a total misunderstanding of the Christian Gospel to call upon the church to preach morality unless the experience of forgiveness and new life in Christ precedes it. Not only is it false to the message of Christ, it is simply a waste of effort. As the biographer of John Wesley put it, in the light of the evidence of what he had observed, 'There is no other means whereby nations can be reformed, than by that which alone individuals can be regenerated.'[28] He had seen the results of faithful, hard-working preachers and pastors, like Charles Simeon and John Wesley who, under God, had called individuals to repentance, faith and new life in Christ. Their changed lives, the fruit of the Holy Spirit, Who had regenerated individual Christians, caused a revolution in our social and political life, as people began to take seriously the importance of obeying God's law.

Although they are not particularly strong, there are signs of hope in the churches of our land, where we might expect to see the beginnings of new life. The crisis which faces our nation should compel all Christians to reassess the quality of their discipleship of Christ and the priorities for their lives on earth, 'while we wait for the blessed hope—the glorious appearing of our great God and Saviour, Jesus Christ'.[29]

The consequence of the resurgence of living Christianity in many parts of Britain at the end of the eighteenth century quickly made its mark on the life of our nation. Today many agree that we stand in need of a similar revolution. Christian morality is not solely concerned with personal values but with standards in public life, with justice and caring for the helpless. The last Conservative Government set up the Nolan Committee on Standards in Public Life and the Labour Party, while in opposition, established (under Sir Gordon Borrie) a Commission for Social Justice. Another more recent example is the Schools Curriculum and Assessment Authority's *Forum on values in schools and the community*. Such actions are good news if they lead to a public debate and ongoing concern for the moral and social condition of our nation.

Christians in public life must participate effectively. They should ask themselves if their speeches and policies really endorse Lesslie Newbigin's assertion: 'I believe the Gospel is truth, and therefore that it is public truth, and therefore that it must determine the kind of society which we seek to nurture.'[30] They might also ask themselves whether they are being heard as distinctively Christian and whether they ever elicit the response that was often given to the Christians who were seeking the abolition of the slave trade. It was asserted that religion should not invade public life because it was a matter of personal choice. On the contrary, the only essential thing needed is that our people once again place themselves under God's law and seek to apply it to public life. Only through the faithful obedience to Christ of his disciples at every level of our society can our nation find again the path to greatness and prove the truth of the proverb that 'righteousness exalts a nation'.[31]

Notes

1. Stalin J. *Marxism and the Colonial Question 1912.* Quoted in Hobsbawn E. Nations and Nationalism since 1870. Cambridge: Cambridge University Press, 1990.
2. Colley L. *Britons – Forging the Nation.* London: Yale, 1992.
3. Latimer H. *Sermons and Remains.* The Parker Society. Cambridge: Cambridge University Press, 1845.
4. Milton J. *Aeropagitica.* Oxford: Oxford University Press, 1875.
5. Psalm 67 v. 1–2. Quoted in NEB Alternative Service Book. Cambridge: Cambridge University Press, 1980.
6. London: The Times 1994, July 4th.
7. Horace. *Odes 2.13.* Oxford: Oxford University Press, 1980.

8. Scott W. *Lord of the Isles*. Edinburgh: Adam and Charles Black, 1852.
9. Owen, W. *Poems*. London: Everyman, 1996.
10. De Tocqueville A. *Religion, Culture and Society*. New York: State University Press, 1994.
11. Deuteronomy 4:6.
12. Proverbs 14:34.
13. Proverbs 25:5.
14. Hooker R. *Of the Laws of Ecclesiastical Polity*. Harvard University Press: Boston, 1977.
15. Burke E. *Reflections on the Revolution in France*. Oxford University Press: Oxford, 1993.
16. Quoted in W G Fallows. *Mandell Creighton and the English Church*. Oxford: Oxford University Press, 1964.
17. Milton J. *Poems*. Warne; London, 1890.
18. Neill S. *The Wrath and the Peace of God*. Cambridge: CLS, 1943.
19. Augustine. *City of God*. London: J M Dent. Everyman, 1945.
20. Scruton R. *Dictionary of Political Thought*. London: Macmillan, 1982.
21. Hebrews 13:14.
22. Newbigin L. *Foolishness to the Greeks*. London: SPCK, 1986.
23. Hookyas R. *Religion and the Role of Modern Science*. Edinburgh: Scottish Academic Press, 1972.
24. Wilberforce W. *A Practical View of the Prevailing Religious System of Professed Christianity in the Higher and Middle Classes of the Country Contrasted with Real Christianity*. London: Cadell and Davies, 1797.
25. Butterfield H. *Christianity and History*. London: Bell, 1949.
26. Davis C. In: *The Loss of Virtue: Moral Confusion and Social Disorder in Britain and America* (Anderson D. ed). London: Social Affairs Unit, 1992.

27. Eliot T.S. *The Idea of Christian Society.* London: Faber, 1939.
28. Southey R. *The Life of Wesley.* London: Longman Brown Green and Longmans, 1846.
29. Titus 2:13.
30. Newbigin L. Unpublished paper, 1994.
31. Proverbs 14:34.

CHAPTER TWO

NATIONAL VALUES—HOW SHOULD THEY BE DETERMINED?

David Cook

Dr David Cook is Director of the Whitefield Institute and Fellow of Green College, Oxford. Dr Cook is well known as a broadcaster through BBC Radio 4's, The Moral Maze. He writes extensively on medical, ethical and theological issues.

'Unless the Lord builds the house, those who build it labour in vain.
Unless the Lord watches over the city, the watchman stays awake in vain.'[1]

On a visit to Toronto, I met several older Canadians who described the threat they felt to their traditional values because of the open immigration policy of the Canadian Government. The irony they expressed was that in the name of Canadian openness, their freedom was now under threat. In the name of tolerance, the national values they held dear as Canadians were no longer tolerated for fear that they offend different racial and cultural groups.

Similar fears have been expressed in the United Kingdom not just with the perceived failure to integrate different racial and cultural groups, but because of the pluralism of moral values. In an age of individualism, it is not fashionable to proclaim or stand for national values, especially if they smack of the past. Our guilt about British imperialism has made us hesitant to express the values which seem to have played a key part in making Britain great. The very presence of variety in moral values has made us hesitant about any and every claim to hold universal values.

At the same time we are in the midst of a rediscovery of communitarian views of society. Such emphases stem from both the right and the left in terms of political philosophy. Political leaders are in the business of offering a sense of the nation and community we are and need to be. In that community we are to care for every member of our society and take our rightful place in the context of the world.

In this chapter, I aim to explore the need for national values; the danger of the wrong kind of national values; the nature and basis of national values; what currently determines such values; and how we might enhance or limit some such determinants as well as facilitate certain key universal, national values.

The need for national values

Before we can discuss how to determine national values, it must be clear that such values are desirable. In an individualistic, selfish society such values will not be popular. They will call into question the self-centredness of much of our personal and social value systems and the ways we live and work.

However, there are two main arguments which can be presented in favour of holding national values. The first is the business of survival. Anarchy is the alternative to shared values. If each does what is right in his or her own eyes,[2] then, as in the days of the Judges in Israel, society will collapse and all of us will be at risk. National values are a key aspect of our survival both as a society and as individual members of that society.

The other reason we need to return to some sense of national values is that individualistic, selfish values have

29

manifestly not worked. Our society is all too often greedy and selfish and our failure as a society to protect the vulnerable and each other against the rising tide of violence, pornography, homelessness, pollution, unemployment, marriage and family breakdown, crime and fear should show us the value of national, universal values.

The wrong kind of national values

The tragic example of the former Yugoslavia and USSR quickly reveals the danger that nationalistic values can create. The disintegration of formerly powerful states into violent conflict between nationalist groupings can all too easily end up with so-called 'ethnic cleansing'. There is a flawed kind of nationalism which seems to hold values based on 'my country right or wrong'. In such cases, genuine morality goes out of the window and every kind of immoral action is justified in the name of national self-interest.

As we seek to consider how national values should be determined, we must reject the parochial nationalism which is nothing more than jingoism and can end up trying to justify the unjustifiable. At a moment in history when the basis of Irish nationalism is under particular scrutiny, it is vital to avoid the wrong kind of nationalism remembering that whatever happens in the Northern Irish scene will have serious consequences not just for the United Kingdom, but especially for the Scots and the Welsh nationalist movements. Patriotism may well be, as Dr Johnson warned, the last refuge of a scoundrel.[3] Nationalistic claims and values must be assessed with great care.

What are national values?

It would make an interesting thesis to explore what values the British nation has had at different moments of history. This is not my intention. It is rather to argue that there are some basic universal values which lie at the heart of all national and public life. These are most clearly expressed in the Ten Commandments.[4] Such values deal with questions of family life, sexual behaviour, the sanctity of life, truth-telling and proper attitudes towards ownership. It is often noted that the Ten Commandments break neatly into two broad categories. The first five deal with humanity's relationship with God. The second five deal with humanity's relationship with each other.

In a world where there are many competing values and value systems, the fact of a common basis of moral values is often overlooked or under emphasised. Yet if we are to survive as people in community we need to have some basic agreed rules for life together. This is why it is no surprise to find in every religious, moral and legal code down through the ages and across the cultures a surprising degree of common ground. That common ground finds its focus in rules about parent-children relationships, sexual behaviour, truth-telling, the value and sanctity of life, and ownership or belonging. Of course, different cultures might express these rules in different ways according to their particular setting or cultural norms. That does not undermine the common base of such values. Indeed, we should expect nothing less given that we are all human and share a common human nature. The universality of human being is matched by the universality of moral values.

We all need to grow up in safety and security and the family, in some form or other, is vital for the well-being of both children and parents. Without such a setting, our life together would disintegrate. Sexual desires and behaviour need to be controlled and regulated. The existence of sexual taboos and rules witness to the benefit and protection such rules provide. If we could not rely on each other's word and had no means of discerning the difference between truth and falsity in speech and behaviour then all social life would collapse. Unless our life was protected and the taking of human life regarded as a matter of the ultimate seriousness, then we would live in fear of each other and spend all our time in the business of self-protection. That would be fine for those of us who were strong and fit enough to survive. The weak and vulnerable would soon be destroyed. Rules about the sanctity of life reveal our human need for protection and proper care of human life. In a society, the ability to draw a distinction between what belongs to me or us and what does not belong seems to be fundamental. The commandment against coveting what belongs to a neighbour is a stark reminder that such a distinction exists and is to be honoured. Appropriate belonging and ownership were clearly part of the social structures not only of Israel, but of other cultures as they struggled into nationhood.

It may seem odd to look to a people who lived so long ago and were a nomadic people at the point they were given the Law; yet Christians, Jews and Muslims recognise that it was God, the creator and Lord of all humanity who was revealing his way and pattern for all humankind in all places and at all times. God's laws are universally valid because human nature is always the same and God's standards remain the same.

The giving of the Law was not for perfect men and women, but for people who had failed to obey God's laws and standards. These rules were for fallen humanity who had to live in a less than perfect world. The laws are minimal laws. They simply tell us what standards are necessary if we are to have any kind of social and national life at all. These laws also carry with them a threat and a promise. The nation which keeps these laws will flourish. The nation which breaks these laws will collapse and destroy itself. Many might well feel that the current state of the British nation is because of a failure to keep God's laws and a reaping of the inevitable consequences of doing our own thing in our own way.

Inevitably these laws simply provide an overarching framework within which it is possible to develop a whole system of laws to cover every detail of life and the complexity of our modern societies. Yet such a framework is vital to act as a basis for the development of such a system of agreed, universal values.

How are national values determined?

It is not possible to cover all the carriers of value and the determinants of national values, but it is possible to note some key ones. We shall examine the role of the family, education, the peer group, the media and the Government. In major ways, these provide a means of determining, supporting or undermining our national values.

The family

The hand that rocks the cradle rules so much of what we think, how we think and the values we all hold. It is fascinating when we are under pressure how often we revert to being like children. The values we learned at our mother's knee come into play when all our other defences are under threat. The problem we are experiencing as a nation is a breakdown of the family and a consequent breakdown of the setting in which family values are taught. Notice this claim is not that all families necessarily lived by the values they proclaimed, but that it was in the family context that such values were taught and propounded. It may well have been a case of doing what was said rather than doing what was done. Nevertheless the values were taught, inculcated and expected to be known and lived by for the younger generation at least.

If this is accurate, then we may reverse the equation and look at the values we see among young people and in society and ask what role the family is playing to arrive at such a state of affairs. A secure and stable family setting does

33

not guarantee that children will all turn out well and become good people and good citizens. It does, however, seem to offer the best hope of arriving at that end. We have not developed a better way of determining the values we need to survive and flourish as a society and nation.

Education

Children all too soon learn that their parents do not know everything and that teachers know better. The move from the home to the school produces a major step in socialisation and in the development of values. It is no accident that, as religious education and religious acts of worship come under increasing pressure in a secularised society, educationalists and governments alike are seeking to plug the gap created. What is called Personal, Social and Moral Education has been wheeled in to try to teach children what values we expect from all members of society. It is in such classes in particular that national values are being taught and developed. It would be wrong to imagine that the teaching of values only happens in those slots on the timetable. In reality every class and every teacher is expressing values in a hundred different ways. Children can pick up the values of adults in all kinds of formal and informal educational settings.

This is why the national curriculum, educational philosophy and teaching methods are so important. They provide a setting and context in which our children are being taught either to be the citizens of tomorrow or to do their own thing regardless of other people. That is one reason why current educational philosophy's emphasis on the rights of the individual is so dangerous. It seems to create a demanding generation who are more concerned about themselves than with their duties and responsibilities to society, family, the nation and the world.

Peer group pressure

We only have to look at the world of fashion to see the impact on all of us of peer group pressure. We are happy to be one of the crowd and insist on dressing and behaving in ways which will help us fit in rather than stand out. For all the much proclaimed individualism of our age, the desire to be acceptable and the same as others seems to be very strong. Yet the crowd is notoriously fickle and fashions change with the direction of the wind. It is to the image makers and fashion and trend setters we must look if we are to understand how values are determined in our society.

The media

The wonder of radio, television and the world of computers has transformed our means of communication and learning. We are all deeply affected by what we watch and the sheer power of visual images assault our senses relentlessly. The problem is that these images are not neutral, but carry particular values and outlooks. We develop our social, personal and national values from the media. Whether it is the papers we read or the programmes we watch and listen to, we are shaped to some extent by what they do to us and the messages they carry. Often we are not even aware of the impact such media actually have, but that in no way belittles the force and success of their role. Those who control the media are in a powerful position to choose and shape our views on issues of the day and to develop our values.

If we take the presentation of news items we can see that careful and conscious editorial work transforms what the public are presented with and the kinds of responses we are likely to make. Selection, emphasis, style and tone can all count as much as the actual content. It is frightening to see how easily an editor can cut a programme or an item in a programme to make a particular point. Such points, once

35

given, are extremely difficult to resist. If we remove the example from the news to the 'soaps', we see the potential for a subtle influence on and shaping of values of many who watch, thinking that they are receiving nothing but entertainment.

Government

It is easy both to underestimate and overestimate the influence that governments can and do play in the creation and supporting of values in a nation. Clearly the law of the land is both an expression of the public will through the representatives of the people and at the same time a vehicle by which public opinion is shaped and led. The influence of the abortion law is but one example of the impact one piece of legislation has had on the attitudes and values of society as a whole. Before 1967, abortion was extremely rare and a subject considered better kept secret. Abortions were exceptional events for exceptional circumstances. Now abortion is in effect on demand and women talk relatively freely about having an abortion. Society, families and many individuals will consider an abortion as little more than having a tooth removed. What began as a permission to perform abortions under certain restricted circumstances has become a situation where abortion is expected by a woman presenting at a clinic. Few seem to be bothered about the significance of what will happen either to the woman or to the life in her womb. There has been a major attitudinal change in the values concerned with abortion and the relative worth attached to the woman's body and her rights and to the rights of the foetus.

Such a brief survey can do no more than indicate the key role in determining the values we uphold as a nation and the means whereby such values may be challenged or reinforced.

36

National values—how should we determine them?

Christians have no right to impose their values on others. They do have a right in a democracy to proclaim their values as forcefully and attractively as possible. They also have a responsibility as citizens to stand for the values which they believe were and are fundamental in the founding and sustaining of the nation. Even more, they have a responsibility before and to God to proclaim and live the standards He has given for all humanity. That means both a proclamation of the minimal values such as those outlined in the Ten Commandments. It is a reminder of the heritage which shaped and made Britain the international power and force for good it has become and continues to be. It also points to the universal values which all men and women everywhere can recognise and affirm. Such values are vital for all of us if we are to flourish as individuals and nations.

However, the Christian has a further obligation and duty. We have thus far only talked of five of the Ten Commandments, that is those dealing with humanity's relationships with each other. The other five are equally if not more important. They deal with God and God's relationship with the humanity He has created. Without a proper relationship with God, many would doubt whether we can fulfil the commandments and certainly would argue that we cannot fulfil our potential to develop our full humanity. That humanity is fulfilled most of all in the incarnation of Jesus Christ. He is the central focus of value for Christians.

The difference between the Old and New Testament values may be summed up crudely as the difference between the minimum and the maximum. The values of the Ten Commandments are minimal standards for the survival of a society. The teaching of Jesus offers the way for each of us individually and together to fulfil our humanity and to grow

37

up into the full personhood that God created us to enjoy. Thus it is that Christians see their role in society as not simply pointing to the basic values for all humankind. They seek to act as salt and light in society, by a prophetic proclamation of God's will and ways accompanied by an incarnation of the values of Jesus in every aspect of life.

However, this does not help us know how to help determine national values in a pluralistic, secularised, God- and Christ-rejecting society. We must begin by a genuine return to the basic universal values which God has given for the whole of humanity. These values can be affirmed by all and recognised as vital for all our well-being. We must also seek to ensure that family life and education from school to university provide settings in which proper values may be taught which enhance human beings rather than diminish us. That will mean offering positive support in the sustaining of families and helping them in the midst of crisis. It will mean a radical re-examination of the role of values in schools, ranging from the national curriculum to religious and personal, social and moral education. It will also mean recognising the way social forces operate and providing positive role models, social opportunities and creative values for all our young people. One possible way forward is to consider some kind of classes in citizenship, not just for the young but for all of us.

The impact of the media and the Government highlights the need for people who are conscious of the need for values to seek careers in the media and in politics. The lack of respect for those in authority is all too often because our leaders do not live in ways which deserve respect. We need a new sense of integrity for those in public life and a return to a sense of vocation and public service rather than self-seeking. With such examples and influences, the whole nation would benefit. It is interesting to recall the national cross-party grief at the early death of John Smith. There seemed little doubt that he was a man of integrity whom our nation could ill afford to lose.

We all need good models and that is true in terms of national values as much as other aspects of life. Until and unless we see such models in operation and are ourselves challenged to emulate and copy them, then we may face still further eroding of the values we need not just to flourish as a nation, but simply to survive.

Notes

1. Psalm 127:1.
2. Judges 17:6.
3. Dr Samuel Johnson. Quoted by Boswell J. *Life of Johnson.*
4. Exodus 20:1–17.

CHAPTER THREE

THE ROLE OF THE MONARCH TODAY

Roger Beckwith

Dr Beckwith is Honorary Librarian and former Warden of Latimer House, Oxford and was previously, Tutor and Chaplain at Tyndale Hall, Bristol. His contribution to Theology and Ecclesiastical Affairs was recognised by the award of a Lambeth Doctorate of Divinity.

It was an unusually open disclosure of her feelings by the Queen, when she called 1992, the year in which the fortieth anniversary of her accession was celebrated, an *annus horribilis*, adding that it was not events but attitudes which had made it such. Her words were a sharp reminder of the way public regard for the royal family has declined over recent years. Few can now remember the way her grandfather led the nation through the years of the First World War, and there are many now who cannot remember the way her father led the nation through the years of the Second World War. But it is not just forgetfulness that has changed attitudes: the Queen's own tireless devotion to duty, still supported by that of the Queen Mother, would have ensured that public esteem remained unchanged, had not other forces been at work. The most influential of these forces, without much doubt, have been television and the press.

The monarchy under scrutiny

The 'power of the press' and the 'public right to know' have been the claims of journalists for generations. But not until very recent times have the statements of journalists been illustrated by living voices and lifelike images on screens in every home. And not until equally recent times have opinion-formers in the media thrown off the restraints of respect for authority, concern for the public interest, sensitivity to the feelings and rights of others, and even decency and reverence, to the extent that we have seen happen in our own day in many areas of journalism and broadcasting. Behind this seems to lie a popular philosophy of hedonism and nihilism, which has done much to undermine remaining Christian ideals, especially among the impressionable young, and threatens to bring about the disintegration of society.

The media, like the trade unions a few years ago, are now tempted to think they are above the law. They try to make and break governments. In Italy recently a press baron even succeeded in making himself prime minister (with disastrous results). In England certain press barons, from home and abroad, have apparently decided to discredit the royal family. They have had considerable success. By ruthless intrusion into private affairs, they have exposed the sexual indiscretions of certain younger members of the family. Having nothing of this kind to urge against the Queen, and relying on the convention that she does not reply to accusations, they have tried to brand her as covetous and inefficient. And, having got this far, they speculate aloud about 'whether the monarchy can survive'. The real question, of course, is whether freedom of speech can survive when it is used with such irresponsibility.

Perhaps, after the needless death of Princess Diana, effective steps will at last be taken to curb the excesses of the press.

The political role of the monarch

The legal doctrine of the sovereignty of Parliament, as popularly misunderstood, makes the monarch a mere figurehead with purely symbolic functions. It is only this that causes the continuance of the monarchy to appear an open question. Yet even if the functions of the monarchy were indeed purely symbolical, they would not for that reason be dispensable. No society can flourish without ideals, and many of the ideals which have influenced Britain for good have their supreme symbol in the monarchy. The ideal of unity, transcending class divisions and political parties, is embodied in the monarchy. So are the ideals of justice and clemency, to which every subject has a right of appeal.

All great acts of state are performed in the name of the crown, the monarch is the commander-in-chief of the armed forces of the nation, and is patron of countless beneficent and charitable services within society. Two recent publications have stressed the great and continuing importance of this aspect of the monarch's work.[1, 2] The symbolism of harmonious family life, which has become so linked with the royal family since the reign of Queen Victoria, and which has been impaired by recent royal separations, divorces and apparent infidelities, is only a small and comparatively modern part of the symbolism with which the monarch is surrounded and identified.

The role of the monarch, however, is *more* than symbolical, and under our present constitutional monarchy this continues to be the case. Whether the English monarchy was ever really absolute is a fair question (Magna Carta and the writings of Hooker suggest the contrary), but even today the sovereignty of Parliament is really the sovereignty of the Crown in Parliament. This is significant, not so much because all parliamentary legislation requires the assent of the monarch (an assent which is now never refused), nor because the Cabinet as the successor of the Royal Council has unique executive powers (powers which it can only exercise so long as it has the confidence of the majority in Parliament), but because the monarch has a continuing and influential personal prerogative, which neither the Cabinet nor Parliament can alienate without constitutional change.[3]

The monarch's prerogative is ill defined, and includes powers sometimes invoked by the Cabinet, but, in so far as it remains personal, Bagehot's description of it as the right to be consulted, the right to encourage and the right to warn, is widely accepted. The regular and frequent meetings between the Queen and the Prime Minister for this purpose are well known. The monarch, on average, has longer experience than any premier, and even so discrete a monarch as our present one can let her displeasure be publicly shown if the premier persists in a policy which she considers sufficiently damaging (as in the case of Mrs Thatcher and our bonds with the Commonwealth).

Members of the royal family other than the monarch can express controversial opinions with much greater freedom, as the Prince of Wales has done in relation to architecture, culture, the environment and the disadvantaged. No one can doubt the influence that his eloquent idealism has exercised, but it is primarily because of his relation to the monarch that what he says is taken so seriously. The monarch has a right to be heard at the very centre of power. And this is not just a luxury of peace-time. The consultative process between the Queen and the Prime Minister today is only a continuation of that between the King and Winston Churchill throughout the war.

The role of the monarch in the Church of England

The monarch is also the supreme governor of the established church.[4] The assertion of this right was the culmination of the struggles between kings and popes throughout the

Middle Ages, which were brought to a head not so much by the marital problems of Henry VIII (a purely English phenomenon) as by the negative reaction of the papacy against the calls, all over Europe, for biblical reform of the Church. The role of supreme governor for the monarch was not without partial precedents, either biblical (in the activities of David, Solomon, Hezekiah, Josiah and other Israelite monarchs) or historical (in the activities of Constantine and later Christian emperors and kings) but, in so far as it was novel, it was a remedy made necessary by the novel errors of Rome.

The Thirty-Nine Articles, drafted by Cranmer in Edward VI's reign and permanently adopted in Elizabeth's, assert the monarch's right to 'the chief government of all estates of this realm, whether they be ecclesiastical or civil', whereas 'the Bishop of Rome hath no jurisdiction in this realm of England'; explaining that, at the same time, 'we give not to our princes the ministering either of God's word or of the sacraments'.[5] The main practical effects of this developed conception of the monarch's ecclesiastical role was that all future church legislation, both in Parliament and in Convocation, was inoperative until it secured his or her assent,[6] and that future appointments to bishoprics were decided by him or her.[7]

The Protestant succession

After the tumults of the Stuart period, further legislative steps were taken in the reigns of William and Mary and of Anne which limited any despotic ambitions which the monarch might have in relation to Parliament,[8] while buttressing his or her supremacy as governor of the church over against Rome. Up to that date, it had not been explicitly required that the monarch should be a member of the national church, and should not rather be a member of the Church of Rome, though this was the natural expectation. It is just about conceivable that the supreme governor

44

of the national church might be of a different religious allegiance, but to be a Roman Catholic would mean that the monarch recognised the Pope as an international governor of the church superior to him or herself, which would contradict his or her own position in the national church as 'supreme under God'.

During the Stuart period, Charles II had been a secret Roman Catholic, and his brother James II had been an open and campaigning one who, like Mary Tudor before him, had made a bid to unreform the national church. It was not of course accidental that, though their father Charles I was a devout Anglican, their mother Henrietta Maria was a Roman Catholic. To prevent these problems ever recurring, the legislation which followed the 1688 Revolution required that future monarchs should not be Roman Catholics or married to Roman Catholics, but should be willing to make an open declaration of Protestantism, and should in fact be members of the national church.[9] William III had been a member of a continental Protestant church (the Dutch Reformed Church) before becoming king, and Anne was married to a Danish prince who had been a member of another continental Protestant church (the Church of Denmark), and Anglicans of this period had no false embarrassment in declaring their Protestantism.

As for the restriction on the monarch being or marrying a Roman Catholic, to represent this as bigotry, in the customary modern manner, is really to forget history and to forget the constitutional position of the monarch in relation to the national church as supreme governor, not supreme bar one.

If the much more appealing public face adopted by the Church of Rome since the Second Vatican Council had been accompanied by any renunciation of previous claims or any apology for previous errors, its relationship to other churches would be very different. Unhappily, however, a church which has claimed infallibility for itself can never renounce anything: the most it can do is to play things down. The claim of Boniface VIII to be the ruler of all monarchs and all mankind,[10] and the consequent action of Pius V in attempting to brand Elizabeth I as a usurper and to release her subjects from their duty of allegiance to her,[11] are not renounced but simply in abeyance for the time being.

The fact that visiting royalty from Protestant countries like England still have to wear black in the presence of the pope, in token of shame, whereas he wears white, is an outward indication of the strict doctrinal limits which, now as before, control Roman diplomacy and inhibit any significant change of attitude on the Roman side.

The supreme governor today

Ever since Convocation was permitted to meet again for business in 1855, and especially since a House of Laity was added to the Houses of Bishops and Clergy under the Enabling Act of 1919, with authority for the resultant Church Assembly to prepare ecclesiastical measures for Parliament, the initiative in church legislation has tended to be taken not by Parliament but by the assemblies of the church. Bishops have continued to sit in the House of Lords, and Parliament's right to initiate church legislation has never been abandoned, but it has become customary for Parliament to content itself with accepting or rejecting measures prepared by Church Assembly or (since 1969) by its successor the General Synod, after receiving advice from its own Ecclesiastical Committee. If it accepts such measures, in both Houses, they go to the monarch for royal assent, and, as with other parliamentary legislation, the assent is never refused.

Under the Synodical Government Measure of 1969, the ancient right of the Convocations of the Clergy to prepare canons of discipline was also transferred to the General

Synod, thus giving the House of Laity a full share in preparing them. Canons go straight to the monarch for royal assent, without being submitted to Parliament, and for this reason are considered to be legally binding only upon the clergy, who alone used to be involved in preparing them. It is rather curious that the laity now help prepare canons to which they are not subject, and it may be that, when synodical government is reformed, the right to prepare them will be returned to the Convocations. However this may be, canons go straight to the monarch, and the monarch's assent is not given so unvaryingly as with measures.

In 1865, Canterbury Convocation prepared five new canons which did not receive the royal assent and so did not come into force (the true facts are as stated by Bishop Kemp,[12] the statements of certain recent law books to the contrary notwithstanding), whereas the last monarch to refuse assent to parliamentary legislation was William III, nearly 200 years earlier. No conflict between crown and Parliament is involved in refusing assent to canons, since canons do not come before Parliament and, now that increasing amounts of controversial legislation are being brought before the Synod, often in the form of measures which authorise the Synod to pass controversial canons, it would seem to be open to the supreme governor to give assent to the measure but to withhold it from the canon, thus arresting divisive action until the church has had time for second thoughts.

The appointment of bishops

The sovereign's role in the appointment of bishops and other dignitaries has long been shrouded in secrecy, the main unanswered question being whether the sovereign ever refuses the prime minister's advice. Under the convention agreed during the Callaghan administration, the prime minister now has two names submitted to him or her by the

Crown Appointments Commission, of which he submits one to the Queen. He or she can, however, ask for two more names, and the question is whether the Queen has a similar veto, as some of her predecessors in this century certainly appear to have had. Speculation is idle, but some believe that the appointment of a much-esteemed Archbishop of Canterbury, well within living memory, was due to the exercise of the royal veto in regard to the first name submitted.

The coronation oath

The sacred status of the monarch in the English constitution is signified by nothing so clearly as by the coronation in church with which his or her reign begins. Central to this service is the coronation oath, the terms of which are determined by statute, and have remained essentially unchanged for the past 300 years. The oath is in three parts, relating to the government of the realm, the execution of justice, and the church. The third part runs as follows:

> Will you to the utmost of your power maintain the Laws of God and the true profession of the Gospel? Will you to the utmost of your power maintain in the United Kingdom the Protestant Reformed Religion established by law?
>
> And will you maintain and preserve inviolably the settlement of the Church of England, and the doctrine, worship, discipline and government thereof, as by law established in England? And will you preserve unto the Bishops and Clergy of England, and to the Churches there committed to their charge, all such rights and privileges, as by law do or shall appertain to them, or any of them?
>
> Reply: All this I promise to do.

This is an oath which relates both to Christianity more broadly and to the Church of England. It says nothing

48

derogatory about other denominations or other religions, but clearly signifies the constitutional position of the monarchy in England as committed to Christianity, to the Protestant Reformation, and to the Church of England as the national church. The ill-considered doubts which two archbishops and, more recently, the Prince of Wales have raised about it have since been wisely withdrawn. The wording is firm but good, and should remain unchanged.

Whether the question which the oath asks about the 'Protestant Reformed Religion established by law' should be interpreted as referring to the (Presbyterian) Church of Scotland as well as to the Church of England is uncertain but quite possible. In 1688, when the phrase was formulated, the Church of Scotland still had its own coronation oath which was sworn by William III the following year. However, since the union of the two kingdoms was completed by the union of the two parliaments and executives, through the Union with Scotland Act (1706), a separate coronation oath has become an anachronism, and an extended meaning can properly be given to the single oath.[13]

The final two questions of the oath relate directly to the Church of England, and contain very specific undertakings. They are clearly intended to put a brake upon unwise change, and ardent innovators in the church need to bear in mind that their schemes could easily conflict with the duty which both church and state have laid upon the sovereign. Necessary adaptation of church practice to changing conditions is one thing, but perversion of biblical doctrine or invasion of legitimate rights is quite another. Charles I and George III are two monarchs on record as finding themselves under pressure from Parliament to break their coronation oath. It would be sad indeed if a monarch of today were ever put under pressure to do this by the church!

The interpretation given to the coronation oath by Mr Justice Lightman in the Williamson case in the Court of Chancery in October 1994 (so far upheld on appeal), that it refers to what is 'currently established' at any particular time, however much it might have been altered by Parliament since the monarch swore the oath, is open to grave objection. It is a comparatively modern interpretation, first proposed by the Whig historian Lord Macaulay in the mid-nineteenth century,[14] and clearly cannot have been current in the time of either Charles I or George III: otherwise, their scruples could easily have been laid to rest. But what is more serious is its effect on the meaning of the oath, for either it makes the oath contradictory, in that the monarch swears to do one thing and then has a duty to do another thing; or else it makes the imposition of the oath upon the monarch an immoral act, since the monarch is required to swear to do he or she know not what—and very possibly to do things which (did he or she but know) would be against his or her conscience. It is very regrettable that this piece of political special pleading should, even temporarily, have been upheld by the courts, and one is grateful to the former Prime Minister for restating in Parliament the historic interpretation: 'The coronation oath is indeed regarded as a solemn undertaking by the sovereign which is binding throughout her reign. Ministers would not advise Her Majesty to sign into law any provision which contradicted her oath.'[15]

Notes

1. Prochaska F. *Royal Bounty: the Making of a Welfare Monarchy.* New Haven: Yale University Press, 1995.
2. Bogdanor V. *The Monarchy and the Constitution.* Oxford: Clarendon Press, 1995.
3. Dicey AV. *Introduction to the Law of the Constitution.* 10th ed. Basingstoke: Macmillan, 1985. Ch 15.
4. Halsbury. *Ecclesiastical Law.* London: Butterworth, 1957. Part 2; Section 2.
5. Article 37.

6. Submission of the Clergy Act, 1533; Act of Supremacy, 1558.
7. Appointment of Bishops Act, 1533.
8. Bill of Rights, 1689.
9. Act of Settlement, 1700.
10. *Unam Sanctam*, 1299.
11. *Regnans in Excelsis*, 1570.
12. Kemp EW. *Counsel and Consent*. Bampton Lectures, lecture 8. London: SPCK, 1961.
13. The situation is not necessarily affected by the re-establishment of a separate parliament for Scotland, since it may have only limited powers.
14. Macaulay TB. *History of England*. First published 1848–1855 (ed. Firth CH, London: Macmillan, 1913–15. Vol. 3, pp. 1411–1412). Quoted by Scales DA. *A Crowning Mercy*. Ramsgate: Harrison Trust, 1996. pp. 10–11.
15. See Hansard for 15th October 1996, volume 282 (Commons), column 585.

CHAPTER FOUR

MORALITY AND THE MARKET-PLACE

James Allcock

James Allcock was formerly Director of Gas Supplies, British Gas plc. He has contributed extensively as a writer and lecturer to the debate on morality and the market-place.

So much has been written about this subject in the last decade that one might be forgiven for thinking that the market was the invention of laissez-faire capitalism in the nineteenth century or even an invention of the British Government in the 1980s. It is not so. There have been markets as long as there have been people.

Need for morality

Neither is morality a new invention. The professorial chairs in business ethics sprouting up all over the place may be new, but it is timely to remember that there is no separate set of moral principles which governs our behaviour in the market-place. To say this is not to despise the study of the application of general moral principles to the business of business. It is as necessary as is the study of the application of moral principles to the business of medicine or competitive sport or any other human and social activity. Indeed, I am going to suggest that there are good reasons for attending to moral questions in the sphere of business relationships and business practice at the present time. This, not only because of a widely perceived breakdown in the moral framework of business affairs, but also because it has from time to time been seriously suggested that the 'good society' would be best promoted by a kind of moral schizophrenia such that we behave immorally at work and morally at home.

Moral questions

I should, for the sake of posterity, explain first briefly why these questions have become so pressing at the present time. There are three principal reasons. First, some of the men, whose names will not matter to posterity, but who never-theless we had been taught to admire as heroes of the market place during the 1980s, bit the dust. The press was full of dawn raids on industrial premises by government inspectors, well-known entrepreneurs fleeing the country rather than face the courts, chief executives of well-respected compa-nies packed off to gaol in disgrace and others merely sunk into bankruptcy. The serious question then became this. Are these just a few rotten apples in a barrel essentially good or are they in truth a fair sample of the business barrel? Is it true after all that the market place is no place for the ethically scrupulous?

Secondly, questions began to arise at a different level altogether at the end of the decade. Since the eighteenth century at least there had been a gladiatorial struggle going on between two systems of thought: between state socialism on the one hand and free market enterprise on the other. Suddenly with the capitulation of the one we were left wondering what we really thought about the other. How proud were we of the free market economy? Had it 'won' because of moral supremacy or just because it was more effective?

Thirdly, the growth of environmental concerns began to

point the finger of suspicion at the short-sighted market economy as the root of the problem because the spoiling of the environment was an 'externality' not costed in the market-place.

It is not the purpose of this essay to evaluate from a Christian point of view the two principal alternative ways of managing economic affairs: the market economy, relying for its allocation of resources on the myriad of individual decisions taken by autonomous players and relying for its driving force on the incentive of personal gain and the private ownership of wealth, and on the other hand, the planned economy where decisions are centralised and taken consciously to promote the common good. That would be a more extensive enquiry than can be undertaken here. Rather it is the intention to establish that it is our business as Christians to be in the market-place and then to enquire into the relationship between morals and the market-place.

Notice first that the market-place as such has no moral personality. It is not and cannot be either moral or immoral. Secondly, notice that the expression is used in at least two different senses. As a pure abstraction it is simply the sum total of the buying and selling transactions that take place in a local, national or international setting. These transactions as such are without moral interest (though the conduct of them is). But it can also refer to a preferred system of organising the wealth-creating activities within any given polity. It is with the market-place in this sense that we have to do.

Christian view of the market-place

We can start by defending the moral credentials of business activity as such in the widest sense from a Christian point of view. The Old Testament suggests that these activities are not only essentially good but are essentially the business of us all. Some would trace this to the image of God in us. Dorothy Sayers, for example:

54

It is observable that in the passage [in Genesis] leading up to the statement about man, [the author] has given no information about God. Looking at man he sees in him something essentially divine but when we turn back to see what he says about the original upon which the 'image' of God was modelled, we find only the single assertion 'God created'; the characteristic common to God and man is apparently that: the desire and ability to make things.[1]

We may prefer to find the justification for our wealth-creating activity in our appointment as stewards. Adam, from the beginning, was to keep the garden and to till it.[2] Everything there (with one important exception) was to be harvested for his own use. Whichever way we choose to take it, the business of business is the fulfilment of our God-appointed role.

But also, business in the widest sense gives us a trinity of experiences in which our likeness to God is identifiable. We are told that he worked and then he rested and then he contemplated with satisfaction what he had done.[3] These are the fundamentals of business life and the trinity of experiences with which we are most comfortable as persons. No two of them will do without the third. So a person is badly wounded if he cannot work (unemployment is always a moral issue), exhausted if he has no rest and deeply frustrated if he has no sense of achievement in his work.

Not only does the business of wealth creation have good moral credentials; it is an important part of our raison d'être. Admittedly, this has not always been the emphasis of Christian teaching. The superiority of monastic asceticism had to be overthrown at the Reformation before our secular calling could find validity and attract prestige. Henceforth the 'religious' and the 'secular' calling could both be the calling of Christian people. Every legitimate calling had exactly the same worth in the sight of God.

Organisation of business affairs

But what of the organisation of our business affairs? It would be surprising if there were not more and less moral ways of setting about it. Some apologists of the free competitive market have sought to defend the market economy on the grounds that it works. I think that a great deal of historical empirical data could be produced in support of that contention.

Brian Griffiths establishes without much difficulty the remarkable record of the market economy in the creation of wealth between 1790 and 1939.

> Throughout the nineteenth century output per person grew at a rate of 1.5% per annum. As a result of the introduction of machines and the growth of markets . . . the standard of living for the average British person—judged in terms of food, clothing, shelter, health, life expectancy, infant mortality, education and material possessions, increased on an unprecedented scale over these years.[4]

Indeed it was the strength of that system that overwhelmed the other and for many people settled the theoretical argument for ever. Critics on the other hand point out that to argue that it works better is not a moral defence at all. For example, John Gray:

> Under market institutions economic growth is maximized and with it the choices available to individuals. This is a weak argument for several reasons. Though the promotion of economic growth may be forced on modern governments by the pressures of political competition in mass democracies, economic growth in and of itself, has no ethical standing.[5]

I am not sure that the pragmatic test is quite so devoid of moral merit as Gray suggests. If one accepts the biblical description of the job we have been given to do, it would seem to follow that the institutional arrangements which fulfil this purpose most successfully have made at least a prima facie case for having the better moral credentials.

Morality and the market-place

Before I finish I shall have to speak of the virtues which must underpin the operation of the market economy. But this is not to give a utilitarian basis to our market place morality. On the contrary, the virtues of honesty and trust and frugality and so on are derived from the same Scripture as our duty and calling as stewards and wealth creators. It would not be surprising if we found that the possession and cultivation of these virtues assisted the fulfilment of our calling.

So, if the problem in economics is the allocation of scarce resources to competing uses, the market through the pricing system and the incentive of personal gain does a good job. Competition stimulates human skill and inventiveness. The incentive of personal gain encourages diligence and energetic activity and the price mechanism signals the strength of preferences for one allocation of resources over another having represented the costs involved in creating alternative goods and services. The decisions that give rise to the resource allocation are numerous and not centralised and the freedom of citizens to choose is maximised. But if all this is true, what is the relationship of morality to the market place and what is the cause of our current sense of unease?

The thesis which gives rise to unease was developed in the eighteenth century by the classical economists. Their view was founded on the observation that since people frequently act in a selfish manner, it is more sensible to build one's economic system on this assumption than rely on unselfishness. But the approach goes beyond this purely pragmatic stance. Self-interest is not just an unpalatable reality but a desirable characteristic to be exploited by a competitive system. Adam Smith's concept of the 'invisible hand' predicted an optimal economic outcome from the interaction of self-interested people acting self-interestedly. Indeed Smith stated that altruistic actions could be less economically beneficial than self-interested ones: 'By pursuing his own interest (a person) frequently promotes that of society more effectively than when he really intends to promote it.'[6]

I cannot in this short essay pursue the economic and philosophical arguments very far but important observations need to be made. First, the proposition was essentially tautological. The most efficient outcome was declared to be that achieved in the market-place by the interaction of individuals who egotistically maximise their own satisfaction. Secondly, even this proposition was held to be true only when certain rigorous assumptions were fulfilled and, as we shall see, they are not in the real world, and this gives rise to most of the moral questions. Thirdly, even if the proposition was sound and the essential assumptions on which its validity rests were fulfilled, the system still subordinates the motivation of people to the results achieved by their interaction. The attempt to talk moral questions out of the market place fails.

But the full flowering of this amoral attitude to economic affairs should be placed where it belongs–in the twentieth and not the eighteenthh century. In the 1980s people too conveniently forgot that Adam Smith had written *The Theory of Moral Sentiments*[7] seventeen years before *The Wealth of Nations*.[6] For him, the pursuit of self-interest was never unrestrained by moral sentiment. If the 'invisible hand' was the hand of God, it was impossible to believe that the will of God should be fulfilled and the welfare of the people maximised by immoral selfishness.

'By acting . . . [morally] we necessarily pursue the most effectual means of promoting the happiness of mankind and

58

may therefore be said in some sense to co-operate with the Deity.'[6]

But by the mid-twentieth century we have a rather different view—from Joan Robinson, one of the most ardent disciples of Keynes: 'It is the task of the economist to . . . justify the ways of Mammon to men. No-one likes to have a bad conscience . . . It is the business of economics, not to tell us what to do, but to show why what we are doing anyway is in accord with proper principles.'[8]

Economics now has broken free altogether from its eighteenth-century roots as a branch of moral philosophy. A modern Christian apologist for the competitive market economy would adhere more closely to the eighteenth-century view. Brian Griffiths for example: 'I am arguing that we should be trying to rescue the market economy from the libertarian philosophy with which it has become entangled and regrettably identified. The market economy has much to offer . . . but only I believe if it is defended within the bounds of Christian justice.'[4]

Framework of moral restraint, obligation and equity

The eighteenth-century thinkers did not intend that the market economy should operate otherwise than in a framework of moral restraint and obligation. But why exactly is it important to insist that the market economy operates within a moral context of restraint and equity?

First, because the belief that the unrestrained operation of self-interest produces a harmonious economic optimum leads to the conclusion that to interfere with the social outcome dictated by market forces or to restrain the incentive of personal gain is to reduce social welfare. This is idolatry. On this view the dictates of the market cannot be gainsaid by considerations of interpersonal obligations or personal behaviour.

Secondly, the secular theory of market optimisation rests on the assumption that the market is 'perfect'. This means a market in which all the players are equally powerful—or rather powerless. But they are not. The use and abuse of market power (monopoly elements in production and distribution and the power of the employers and the unions in the labour market), the inequality of relevant information known to parties to a transaction and the different purchasing power available to parties with different resources, all give rise to the fundamental need for both social legislation to interfere shamelessly with the market equilibrium which would otherwise arise and a moral framework of honesty and trust and mutual obligation if a free competitive market is to work in a justifiable way. And the control of monopoly and fraud and even competition will almost certainly require the codification of relevant parts of the moral framework in statute law. The readjustment of so-called market optimisation is important not only within a single polity but in order to seek a just distribution of wealth between nations. If space permitted the centrality of these issues could be illustrated over and over again.

Thirdly, whether or not you believe that the 'prisoners' dilemma' establishes that co-operation rather than selfishness is necessary for optimal results, it is clear that our transactional activities have consequences which are not evaluated in the transaction itself. Economists call these ' externalities'. The potential destruction of beautiful landscapes, the profligate use of irreplaceable resources, the pollution of rivers and the atmosphere are legitimate concerns which give us the right to constrain the freedom of parties to make commercial exchanges which have these attendant disadvantages.

Fourthly, moral restraint is necessary to put limits to the extent to which people may be enticed into commercial transactions or motivated to indulge in unprincipled behaviour. Two examples may suffice, advertising and performance related pay. Advertisement is entirely necessary to the working of a competitive market economy which depends on suppliers making competing claims on our disposable income. Yet advertisement must be constrained by the need for truth and decency. Similarly, the incentive of personal gain is central to the working of a market economy. Yet, there must be a limit beyond which this motivation may not be further inflamed. To pay policemen more, the more convictions they obtain, may do wonders for their standard of living but may serve the cause of justice a good deal less well.

Finally, precisely because all players in the market-place are not equally well equipped to play, the distribution of income and wealth is very unlikely to be equitable. There must be compassion in society for 'the alien and the father-less and the widows' but also for the stupid and the luckless. It may well be urged that in a market economy underpinned by an adequate moral conscience the redistribution should be voluntary and not by taxation. That is a separate question. The main point is to assert that we must not hesitate to rearrange for moral reasons the distributional outcome which an unfettered market would bring about.

But is it not enough to insist that the economy operates within an adequate legal framework? In the first place law is, or should be, the expression and codification of an accepted moral order. But secondly, law is not flexible enough to replace and render unnecessary a commonly perceived moral order in the market place. I wish I had space to illustrate the truth of this from my long experience of the negotiation of major contracts. Where there is no trust about intention it is almost impossible to draft a contract which is not open to widely different interpretation. Where there is no sense of moral obligation to comply, it is virtually impossible to draft legislation without loopholes to be exploited.

None of this is to say that our perception of what is fair is unchanging. For the Christian the source of our moral

61

precepts is the revealed word of God and that does not change. But society will take different views about their application from time to time. Consider the following: the purchase of commissions in the Services; the purchase of seats in Parliament; trading shares on the basis of privileged information; the purchase of private education and the purchase of private health care. All of these have at some time been regarded as proper things to purvey in the market place. The first two have long been illegal, the third has only recently become illegal and the other two are still allowed. All these judgements could be challenged. Are the troops now better led? Are we now more wisely governed? Can there ever be equality of information in capital markets? Should we be able to buy the inside track to good education or even to life itself?

There is a certain smugness about the glee with which commentators and historians trace the collapse of the Russian soviet system of government and economic management. We would be better advised to attend to the signs of decay in our own. A competitive market economy will not long survive the destruction of the moral framework within which it operates. At least, it may survive but only as an unprincipled jungle. There will be no defence of our freedoms of action and of choice. There will be no equity or compassion. It will not be kept within 'the bounds of Christian justice'.

Conclusions

Our economic arrangements have rested for centuries on the bedrock of the Judaeo-Christian ethic. If it is right to say that our secular calling as businessmen in the widest sense, defended and expounded at the Reformation, finds its origin either in our likeness to God as Creator or in the Biblical ordinance to subdue and to steward the natural creation, is it possible that the Judaeo-Christian moral framework can be replaced by another? The purpose of our secular work (and therefore the operation of the market place) and the moral underpinning of that activity have the same origin in the Biblical revelation. But the Christian ethic will not long survive if it is finally detached from an intellectual confidence in the truth of the Judaeo-Christian revelation.

Christian dogmatics are everywhere ridiculed in society. At the same time we strive by exhortation and the multiplication of regulatory agencies to discipline the market-place. This cannot succeed. Suppose that by the time the Club celebrates its bicentenary the developing economies of the Far East have achieved a material prosperity which puts the European industrial revolution in the shade—and they do it on the basis of a Buddhist ethic—what shall we then say? It seems to me that we will either have to say that there is a similarity in the *relevant* ethical principles, or that we were rash to claim for Christendom exclusively the source of those freedoms, disciplines and senses of obligation on which, I have argued, the operation of an acceptable market economy depends.

When Jesus drove the money-changers from the Temple, accusing them of turning it into a den of thieves, he meant neither that commercial activity was intrinsically evil nor that all commercial operators were dishonest. I am sure he did mean that there is a proper place for worship and a proper place for work. Christians are to be involved in both but must not confuse the one with the other. If we must worship in spirit and truth, we must work in spirit and in truth as well. A market place which wholly lacks the fragrance of the Temple is no place for Christians to be and no place for any to enjoy.

Notes

1. Sayers D. *The Mind of the Maker.* London: Methuen, 1941.

2. Genesis 2:15.
3. Genesis 1:31–2:3.
4. Griffiths B. *Morality and the Market Place*. London: Hodder and Stoughton, 1982.
5. Gray J. *The Moral Foundations of Market Institutions*. London: Health and Welfare Unit. Institute of Economic Affairs, 1992.
6. Smith A. *The Wealth of Nations*. London: Methuen, 1961.
7. Smith A. *The Theory of Moral Sentiments* (Raphael DD, Mackie AL eds). Oxford: Clarendon Press, 1976.
8. Robinson J. *Economic Philosophy*. London: G A Watts & Co, 1962.

CHAPTER FIVE

THE VALUE AND PURPOSE
OF EDUCATION

Richard Wilkins

Richard Wilkins is General Secretary of the Association of Christian Teachers and was formerly a teacher in Primary, Secondary and Further Education.

The Chief Rabbi, Dr Jonathan Sacks, once reminded an audience representing diverse faiths of the importance of education in Judaism. He traced this as far back as the Exodus, to the most critical events of Israel's deliverance from slavery. In the final plagues to which God subjected the Egyptians, in the climactic Passover visitation, and in the overthrow of Israel's pursuers in the Red Sea, one abiding purpose of God throbbed like a drum in Moses' ear: you shall tell your children what happened here, and you will tell them what it means.[1]

Central to the practice of Israel's faith was the obligation to tell its children about God's mighty acts in history. Dr Sacks twice illustrated this abiding principle in Jewish life. Referring to the formative period of rabbinic Judaism, he told how the rabbis ruled that a Jewish community that did not provide a school should be excommunicated. Secondly, to show later Judaism's exaltation of learning over ceremonial, he cited a rabbinic saying that a wise man of illegitimate birth was greater than an ignorant high priest.

The role of education

The role of education in preserving a community and empowering it to meet new challenges is thus rooted in the Scriptures which Jews and Christians share. Christian history provides examples of a passion to learn and to teach. More than once Christians have out-thought and out-argued their opponents. They have emerged as fearless researchers and conscientious teachers. Spiritual revival has often led to the expansion of popular education. The Reformation both liberated the Church laity and also called it to personal responsibility in the light of the written word of God, so that the acquisition of literacy became a sacred duty and education a means to that acquisition.

With such an inheritance and reviewing the challenges of our own time, we can assess the value and purpose of education in the UK today.

The role of schools

While it is a great mistake to confine the meaning of education to the process of schooling, schools are, nevertheless, usually seen as the chief instruments for educating a society. At certain times (and this is one such time) penetrating questions are asked about whether schools as we have known them are, or ever have been, efficient educators of the general population. These questions are serious, and alternatives to schooling must be taken seriously. However, the persistence of schooling despite these questions suggests that societies need them. Indeed they do, for reasons such as the following.

Schools are symbolic

Emile Durkheim, the father of modern sociology, said that schools represent a secular society's best view of itself.[2] Schools have eclipsed churches as the institutions that

66

embody society's ideals. Society's hope for the future lies no longer in sacred buildings but rather in those secular buildings in which the young are trained according to their elders' ideals. Society rests its hopes in the means of preparing the younger generation for progress beyond the attainments of its predecessors. Just as Israel's faith generated schools out of the belief in the earthly destiny of the chosen people, so secular humanism expresses in policies of universal schooling its belief in the infinite improvability of human beings in the relay race of earthly life.

A nation puts into its schools not only its children but also its conscience. It hopes for the best in the children it sends to school, and it demands extraordinary virtues in their teachers. Honesty, fidelity, altruism, faith and patriotism are expected to irradiate the life of schools, and if they do not there is outrage among parents and politicians who might find those virtues a tiresome drag on their own adult ambitions. Linguistic immaculacy and accurate arithmetic are demanded in schools by a society that speaks and writes with a salesman's licence, while making two and two equal three in a competitive tender and five in a final invoice. Why? Because, as Durkheim said, schools exist to symbolise the standards we honour but seldom achieve.

Schools are convenient and safe

In a powerful essay, Professor David Hargreaves outlined the kind of education which is made possible by modern technology.[3] The juvenile day-barracks could be replaced by local learning networks in which teenagers equipped with laptop computers could gather information by modem at home, and range throughout their communities learning from the real life that they observed. In that way they would prepare their minds for adult life with a sense of proportion and perspective derived from the outside world rather than the reverse-telescope world visible from the school. He had to admit that this prospect was clouded by what he called 'the custodial function of schools'.

When compulsory attendance at school was first introduced in the 1870s it was unpopular because children's earning power was curtailed. Later, in times of high employment, the need for children to be cared for at school while both parents worked was essential. Now, with unemployment of one or both partners creating some domestic traumas (especially when dad is the one whom no employer wants), there is relief from the angry, desolate days while the children are at school. Single parents are even more dependent on their children being looked after at school while they carve out a meaningful life.

We have become accustomed to our young being confined to youth reservations for large parts of the day. Truancy is, quite rightly, seen as a possible apprenticeship to crime. At least as important as anything that the children might do or not do in school is the fact that they are there and are someone else's responsibility, while adults get on with their lives.

Schools provide rites of passage

The role of a school in marking progress into adult life is not prominent in our consciousness. Our appreciation of this element in schooling is obscured by the differences of prestige among schools; we have no nationally shared road to adulthood. It is not my purpose here to argue that we should have such a common experience. Nevertheless, within the shared understanding of a social or professional class, or a neighbourhood, the shared experience of a particular school marks, at least by its ending, a certain coming of age. Perhaps the Americans, with a more general school terminology, relate more nationally the landmarks of school education to those of growing up. Graduation from (as distinct from dropping out of) 'high school' may be not only an academic but also a civic *bar mitzvah*.

68

The only way in which our education system transcends its own differences to give a national accolade of maturity is by qualifications. To have acquired the appropriate sixteen-plus certificates is to show by that means, in the absence of any other, that some kinds of growing have so far been completed. Concern that young people leave school 'without qualifications' is mainly due to a worry that they have no competence. But it is partly due also to an anxiety that they have no identity in the public eye and no sense of self-worth. A desire for national qualifications which everyone achieves arises at least in part from a wish that young people emerge correctly processed for employment, higher education, and with a recognition of being worth something.

Education is essential

Schools are the most obvious evidence of education in a modern society. Education and schooling are not identical, but the three roles of schools examined above show some causes of schools' durability. Modern society with its changing employment opportunities, its shifting family patterns, and its need for factories of hope, builds schools. It could not do otherwise without revolutionary consequences.

My stating of these reasons for schooling might seem disappointing, and even cynical. They do, however, show why a system of education based on schools can survive the jading of idealism and endemic disillusionment with schools' efficiency. Schools paradoxically seem to benefit and promote many individuals without having much provable effect on the overall tone of society. On the contrary, the overall tone of society, derived from non-educational motives, seems to act powerfully on schools for change or inertia. We can, however, move from this sedimentary foundation to look at education in more genuinely hopeful, idealistic and spacious ways.

The fact that much rhetoric about education is less

genuine than it sounds must not make us think that ideals, hopes and progress are always illusions. As we saw at the beginning, God's choosing of a people involved His affirmation that education is essential. So encouraged, we can look positively at education, in and out of school, in terms of its essential features and with reference to the modern world.

What education means

We need to grasp the meaning and essential functions of education to evaluate its purpose and performance. There are functions built into education which are performed more or less inevitably. It is as well for these to be consciously articulated and, if possible reconciled in theory, policy and practice. Failure to do that helps to explain why £469 million was spent on an English National Curriculum that had to be binned before it had been fully introduced.

Education tells young people what adults think is important

This must strike awe into designers of school curricula. If they really want the curriculum to cover everything adults believe to matter in life, and accurately to reflect adult priorities, they must take the consequences. Conversely, if reading, numeracy, spelling and grammar really do have the life and death quality with which schools are asked to invest them, the adult society which children observe ought to reflect the same priorities.

There are matters such as some aspects of religious, political, economic, moral and sex education which schools cannot handle for fear of offending parents. If so, pupils have a right to know that these matters are ones for which adults struggle, fight and die, and that they are so important that they cannot be examined in school. How they get information about them is open to discussion. Such a message requires the school humbly to renounce the right to say what is or is not important knowledge. But if it cannot cope with potentially inflammatory topics it has no honest alternative but to admit its inadequacy. If this limitation was acknowledged openly, attitudes to religion communicated by school curricula would be very different.

Adult educators go through severe self-doubt in times of rapid social and technological change. In education, teacher confidence is half the battle, and it is difficult for the adult who grew up in an obsolescent age to be confident in front of children who are closer to the age that is to come. The cure, I earnestly believe, is a knowledge of history. Sir Winston Churchill's view that the farther back we look the farther forward we are likely to see is profoundly true. To know the past is to become accustomed to change; the greatest obstacle to facing the future is not knowledge of the past but enslavement to a present in which we have vested interests.

Having said all this, communication of traditional basic skills and values of a culture are essential in a programme of education. They are not only useful for livelihood and citizenship but vital for identity. There is every reason to believe that much higher general levels of literacy, numeracy and scientific knowledge will be needed in any foreseeable state of civilisation. A moral and religious framework, with a sense of being valued and of belonging, needs somehow to be put before today's children as never before. One of the most exciting and challenging educational opportunities in the education of Britain's multi-racial, multi-religious population is, I believe, a sense of common nationhood.

Education enables children to make sense of life now

Since the 1960s, a number of very self-conscious youth cultures have come to prominence. These have expressed a refusal to accept the prevailing adult view of life. Education cannot succeed unless it seems to matter to its clients now. That does not mean surrender to their short-sighted whims.

It means, rather, devising strategies which harness the information that we know students will need in future to their present emotional needs at various stages of development. Underlying all those needs is the basic need to feel secure. Those who get feelings of security from gathering information may become academics. Those who get security out of solving problems may become various kinds of learned and scientific professionals and technicians. Unless a programme of education is ruled by moral purpose and a clear world view, those who need security will find it in less acceptable occupations.

If security is so important, it follows that experiences of failure, while necessary for a realistic understanding of life, have to be rationed carefully. Failure may provoke us to sterner efforts of improvement. It may also alienate us, and convince us that adult values are hostile. Education that works will offer experience of real, not bogus, achievement. Failure is particularly painful to young people trying to establish their identities. Educators must strive to prevent failure among their students. The value of failing is most obvious to those who watch other people doing it while they themselves succeed.

Education is 'prophetic'

This is obviously true in the popular sense of foreseeing the future, but it is true also in some of the ways in which the Bible depicts prophecy.

First, education, like prophecy, relates responsible action now to an imminent future. A view of the future which is suffused by a sense of accountability to God is the only one that Christians can fully accept.

Secondly, education is directed at both the individual and the community. Like prophecy, it is offered in the hope of a corporate change of mind and direction, but in ministering corporately it must allow for individual response. Education

72

cannot be predicated on a programme that will only work if everyone does the right thing.

Thirdly, education conveys moral values, whether or not it tries to do so. That is obviously the case in the content of the teaching and style of relationships. It is also true in the ways 'the system' works. Money is not the measure of all things, but if primary schools need more funds and yet are permanently funded less than secondary schools, something is said about the value placed on young children's education. If children who go by default to unpopular schools have a worse education than those who go to popular schools, the cause and effect relationship is morally reversed; those children are worth less, so they deserve a poorer education. The prophets denounced that way of evaluating disadvantage.

Fourthly, education, like prophecy, is too big to be contained within the buildings and institutions that represent it in the community. The religion of the biblical prophets overflowed and broke out of the Temple, the priestly caste, the synagogue and the scribes, and came also out of the mouths of fig growers and fishermen. Children learn during the many hours that they are not in school, from people and media not connected with official 'education'. The implications of this include the need to establish a learning society where standards of adult work, scholarship and morality are assessed in terms of their example to the young. Tabloid newspapers may sell, but what do they teach? Education must also be recognised as 'charismatic', in that children might learn most from respected and loved but uncertificated parents, tradesmen and story-tellers. Education's greatest impetus comes in the home. No school can compensate, even academically, for the family.

Fifthly, education involves leadership. None of the enabling, facilitating and supportive, non-directive consultation can get anywhere without someone in charge of it who knows where the child, the community and the world are going. Leadership in education is the ability to bring the

73

grand vision into focus on a single practical choice and a desirable, perhaps difficult, effort of will. The teacher prophesies when s/he teaches a child to read a book or a computer screen, because the child must make its way in a world where information is in print.

Leadership requires that decisions be made in the light of reality not yet seen. The moral element again comes to the fore. True education enables us to see that honesty is the best policy, that love endures and prevails over all things, and generosity makes sense. Our present adult society does not teach these lessons. Only by the grace of God working through true educators, official and unofficial, will children learn that these things are so.

Conclusion

In the fiftieth year after the discovery of the Nazi death camps, I was impressed by a part of Claudia Koonz's book *Mothers in the Fatherland*.[4] She interviewed German women who had risked their lives to help Jewish neighbours and vulnerable opponents of the regime, asking them how they made their decisions to become 'resisters'. All were surprised to be asked; at least one could not understand the question. 'What else could we do?' they asked. 'It was unthinkable not to help those poor people. There was no alternative.' Their answers lacked philosophical sophistication, but somehow or other their moral educators had succeeded. Only education like that can give conviction to our passionate cry at the sight of Auschwitz: 'Never again.'

Notes

1. Exodus 12:24–27.
2. Durkheim E. *The Elementary Forms of Religious Life*. New York: Free Press, 1995.

3. Hargreaves D. *The Mosaic of Learning*. London: Demos, 1994.
4. Koonz C. *Mothers in the Fatherland: Women, the Family and Nazi Politics*. London: Methuen, 1987.

CHAPTER SIX

THE IMPORTANCE OF THE FAMILY

John Tripp

Dr John Tripp is Senior Lecturer in Child Health at the Postgraduate Medical School, University of Exeter and Consultant Paediatrician at the Royal Devon and Exeter Hospital. His major research interests are the family and sex education.

What is a family?

The many common patterns of family structure in the second half of the twentieth century have made 'family' increasingly difficult to define; rapid changes in the people that are both included and excluded by different definitions have meant that the concept of the nuclear family (two married parents and their children) has less utility. A major problem for those interested in the needs of families has thus been a semantic one: that of being able to define the parameters of a family without excluding many of the different family structures in which adults and children now live. At the risk of alienating some readers I would like to attempt a working definition of 'The Family' at the beginning of this chapter on which to base subsequent discussion.

Families include a group of people linked by genetic and or emotional relationships. The closer these ties, the greater the degree of interdependence and responsibility that exists between members. Family ties exist across generations and family relationships are permanent throughout the lives of each of the individuals, often exerting their influence even after death. Additions to families, other than births and adoptions, are most common as a consequence of an adult forming a personal relationship with a family member; this also establishes a new link between two families. While a legal contract of marriage has often been regarded as part of the definition of a family, many would argue that the permanent commitment of two partners to each other has the same force and effects. Additions to a family by marriage, or cohabitation, have in recent decades become both more frequent and more complex; the formation of step families means that some relationships are superseded by new, theoretically identical ones, with double representation of some relatives.

Characteristics and functions of families

The essential characteristics of family seem to include the permanence of these human relationships (as distinct from those of friends, teams or work-place associates), exclusivity (in that it is not possible to join a family except by prescribed routes), commitment to each other (as exemplified by parent—child and marital relationships) and loyalty (so that the above qualities usually withstand stresses which would terminate other relationships).

Families that have these characteristics have been widely regarded as providing a number of important functions in our society. They are the basic units of society which provide a stable environment for procreation, the nurture of children and mutual support for all members. They enable the continuity of a society where personal values, morality and 'good citizenship' can be passed on to future generations.

What is happening to the family in the UK?

While we tend to think of recent changes in families as most marked in relation to out-of-wedlock childbirth, separation and divorce, other influences include later child-bearing, an overall reducing birth rate and changes in adult relationships across generations.

The fall in the birth rate has been significant though not as great as in some other European countries. A growing proportion of women choose not to conceive; there has been recent concern about the advisability of carrying out sterilisation procedures for women in their early twenties who do not believe that they will ever wish to become pregnant.

There has been an increase in the social and geographical mobility of adult children resulting in less dependence on parents in middle life. The existence of the welfare state and the improvements in residential provision for the elderly and the disadvantaged have meant a gradual but steady progress towards decreased responsibility by children for the care of their ageing parents. The increase in the number of elderly (particularly very elderly) people over recent decades and the inability of the welfare state to continue to fund their care will require a reversal of this trend.

The advent of national health and social services introduced concepts of good health and good parenting practices. Doctors and other professionals assumed new roles in the setting of 'norms' and had profound influences on social policy.

Violence in the family

It is recognised that children and adults are most likely to experience violence and even murder within families. Family members are most likely to subject a child to abuse, whether emotional, physical or sexual. It is, therefore, within families that people experience not only the closest but also the most personally threatening relationships. While child abuse is a legitimate ground for public intervention in family life, it is now recognised that the alternative of institutional or foster care is often more problematic for children than a sub-optimal family environment. Family ties are extremely robust and in contrast to previous practice it is now professional policy that, wherever possible, family relationships should be maintained and supported. Such a policy, while containing an element of risk for those children who might otherwise have been taken into care, is believed to maximize the chances of their successful integration into society.

Political and economic influences on the family

A number of economic changes, both of policy and climate, some associated with the introduction of the welfare state, have weakened both the independence and economic stability of the family.

Family economics

Rising female employment has become a necessity rather than a choice for many families (see below) and the fact that women are much more likely to achieve full employment in a family where the man is in work has accentuated differences between the 'haves' and 'have nots', the rich and the poor. The rise in unemployment was particularly acute for males seeking to achieve full-time employment sufficiently well paid to support a family, while in contrast there has been a major increase in low paid, part time and often temporary jobs, particularly for women.

During recent decades a steadily increasing proportion of the population have become house owners, and on several occasions there has been rapid inflation of house prices. In recent years the combination of redundancy for bread-winners and negative equity for householders has become more common; this has placed enormous financial strain on many middle and low income families, undoubtedly contributing to stress in relationships.

The UK government, in common with those of many other industrialised countries, has changed the tax and benefit systems, both to give greater equality between men and women, and to encourage women supported by benefits to take paid work. Separate taxation for couples, reduced married persons' allowance and the present benefits system, together with tax disregard of a single parent's earnings, mean that a single mother will usually be financially better off if she remains without a live-in partner. This severely disadvantages low earning two parent families whose marriages are likely to face the greatest pressure.

Similarly, the benefits system currently appears to provide disincentives for family bread-winners to seek paid work; disposable family income for a couple in rented accommodation with two children is effectively taxed at 98% for all earnings between £15 and £190 per week. While this latter policy may not make families poorer, since they have access to benefits, the disincentive to work may exacerbate male unemployment; this has severe 'knock-on' effects on male self-esteem and in turn on men's ability to function effectively as fathers.

Suggestions that fiscal policies which disadvantage married couples with children may have negative effects on family stability are often dismissed. There are no data to confirm that we can safely ignore the possibility; it may be that the onus should be to disprove the existence of perverse effects rather than presume that there are none.

Marriage

The aspirations of adolescents and young adults appear to have altered little in the face of dramatic changes in family stability and there are few who do not hope for a long-term relationship with another adult, the possibility of raising children and a stable family. These three parts of marriage have now become dislocated from each other; sexual relationships can be independent of a permanent relationship and carry very little expectation of pregnancy; the commitment to a relationship clearly expressed by cohabitation is neither permanent nor linked to procreation. There is widespread ignorance among cohabiting couples of the very significant legal rights accorded to a cohabiting father in relation to property and his lack of rights in relation to parenthood.

Conception outside marriage

As far as chronicled British history allows examination of the question, a significant number of conceptions have always occurred before marriage; that fact is often quoted by historians and others as evidence that, taking a long-term view, little has changed. Before reaching such a conclusion however, it is necessary to look beyond the crude statistics and in so doing we find fundamental differences in out-of-wedlock child-bearing. In the seventeenth century there was a real problem for demographers in establishing who was legally married though this was not an issue for the couples concerned, whose permanent bond defined the nature of the relationship. Since formal censuses began the extra-marital birth rate remained around six per cent of live births right up until the mid twentieth century; now this is over thirty per cent. While previously there were clear expectations either that marriage would precede pregnancy, or that child-bearing would result in marriage, these no longer apply. A sexual relationship during cohabitation, with or without pregnancy, is now a normal precursor of marriage; child bearing carries no automatic link with marriage.

81

Cultural influences

In examining families in the UK, it must be remembered that the multi-cultural nature of our society, where ethnic and religious groupings have particular significance, means that population generalisations mask potentially major and important differences between subpopulations; it is not proposed to discuss these in detail in this chapter. The ways in which partnerships are formed vary considerably, from the continuing major importance of parental choice of their children's partner in many Asian and Muslim communities, to the expectation in some Afro-Caribbean groups that permanent marital relationships are formed after, rather than before, pregnancy (this latter situation is also common in some northern European countries such as Iceland and Sweden). Again in both the European and Afro-Caribbean cultures where such practice is common, or even the rule, parenting was, traditionally, associated with family formation. Children whose family culture is significantly influenced by religious belief (whether practising Christian, Muslim, Jew, Hindu or Buddhist) will face major conflicts of belief and behaviour between their families' expectations of them, those of their peers and the family values that they see portrayed in the media.

The emancipation of women

There is little doubt that the emancipation of women has made very significant differences to both men and women's expectations of marriage. Increased opportunity for women in employment has, for more able women, resulted in their being able to enter what was previously a male domain. This has brought with it fulfilment of many women's expectation of being able to enjoy the stimulation and satisfaction of professional or other careers which are not terminated by marriage. A greater number of women are now able to be less dependent on men since, with their own income, they no longer need to marry in order to finance a family or, having married, they can survive with much greater ease, both financially and socially, without a partner.

Associated with these important developments, other, perhaps unforeseen, changes have taken place. The majority of women in employment are not in professional or managerial jobs but are in unstimulating, poorly paid, low status and part-time employment. Instead of a freedom to achieve independence there is for many a requirement to work, often in these unrewarding jobs, in order for their relationship and family to avoid relative poverty. At the same time this reduces opportunities for parents to spend time with their children, or even regularly to share meals together.

A second consequence is that in many relationships there is either the expectation that both partners take a much more even share of the household tasks and responsibilities or that the woman needs to be a successful lover, spouse, mother, housekeeper and bread-winner all at the same time. A woman who is able to fulfil these expectations gains the approbation of her partner, her work colleagues and her peers. In contrast if a man is willing and able to meet the needs of the partnership by undertaking a number of household tasks, he is likely to receive reinforcement only from his partner. Thus, while women have been largely successful in taking on male roles, which are seen to be of high status and value (to an extent limited only by male dominance and power in the work-place), men have been less willing (or able?) to take on women's roles in the home, which are perceived as being of low value and status.

The overall result has been an unplanned and unwitting devaluation of child rearing in a culture where children already have a lower priority in the everyday life of adults than they do in many other European countries and other cultures.

It has been suggested that links between psychology and biological differences between men and women are responsible for the lack of success by society in achieving not only equality of opportunity, but equality of family roles for men and women. Since there are obvious biological differences of function by gender, it could be argued that similar psychological differences should be presumed until proved otherwise; the reverse situation currently operates.

The interdependence of husband and wife, which has always been a fundamental part of the marriage contract, has thus now changed. While the interdependence continues and is perhaps even increased, it is no longer between two people with defined and different roles, but between two people each with potentially identical roles. The requirement is to divide responsibilities, not on the basis of accepted societal norms, but in an individual way for each relationship, so that there is no recourse for either partner to normative experience. This alteration in men's and women's roles may thus be associated with another change in marriage, which is that cohabitation and marriage relationships are now more often of a companionate nature, based primarily on love, rather than a partnership structure based on a contract.

The difference is about more than issues of work and home-making: equality of opportunity and expectation are now fundamental in many relationships. It extends to sexual behaviour, where the Victorian acceptance that intercourse should be endured for the husband's pleasure has been replaced by heightened mutual expectation of sexual expertise and enjoyment. In a companionate marriage there is more emphasis on each partner's expectations from the relationship and less on the duties and responsibilities that each are accepting as part of a contract in a family partnership. The birth of children emphasises these changes, requiring a change of focus which can cause stress in the relationship. The new focus may necessitate either

84

complex and sometimes impossible roles to be fulfilled by the woman and/or a major change in the family role of the man.

At the same time, there remains in society a double standard in relation to sexuality which is perhaps most marked in adults' expectation and acceptance of their adolescent children's sexuality. Parents exercise far less control over adolescent boys than girls and are much more likely to accept the possibility that boys will be sexually active in early adolescence, despite the likelihood that their partners will be younger. Consistent with greater gender equality, double standards in relation to infidelity are less marked than in previous generations.

Separation and divorce

While marriage is the hope of most young people and is achieved by the vast majority in Britain, both the outcome and the general expectations of marriage have changed dramatically over recent decades. In England almost four in ten first marriages will end in divorce, as will half of all subsequent marriages. These figures take no account of the number of cohabitations that end in separation and thus grossly underestimate the rate of breakdown of 'permanent' relationships. Recent evidence from national statistics suggest that marriages preceded by cohabitation are significantly more likely to end in divorce. These startlingly high numbers should not be allowed to mask the fact that the majority of first marriages (over sixty per cent) continue throughout the lives of both partners.

Reasons for the dramatic increase in separation and divorce are notoriously difficult to elucidate, but there is a general belief that the major liberalization of the law in relation to divorce has followed, rather than caused, the increased rate of marital breakdown. Data for this assumption are difficult to obtain. Information about marital breakdown and separation in countries where there has been no liberalisation of divorce law should give useful clues. The Republic of Ireland is an example of a country where there is a high rate of de facto separations; the different religious milieu of a strongly Roman Catholic community makes direct comparison difficult.

Another view is that marriage is no less successful than in previous generations, but that unsatisfactory relationships can now be publicly and legally ended while before they had to be endured in private. A further hypothesis is that more marriages today end by separation rather than death simply because, on average, they now last longer. However, the average length of marriage in the UK has remained unchanged for over a century. To suppose that the present trends are simply the result of marriages lasting longer, one would have to hypothesise that fate determined that most marriages that would today be unsuccessful were in the past likely to be ended by death.

Variation in family forms

These major changes in the formation and dissolution of families, originally consisting of two natural parents and children, have largely accounted for the explosive increase in other family forms, with twenty-one per cent of children now living in single-parent families and eight per cent in reconstituted families of various forms.

Lone parent families

A larger proportion of children will experience a single parent family than is suggested by these figures. Only a minority of children are brought up in *always* single families since lone mothers whether never married, previously married or cohabiting on average only remain single for relatively few years of their children's lives. Lone parent families form the largest identifiable group of socio-economically deprived individuals and are particularly likely to be caught in the 'benefits trap'. Single parents find it difficult to obtain work that is sufficiently well paid to enable them to afford child care.

Children whose parents divorce will almost universally experience a period of significant economic disadvantage which, while usually relative to their previous expectation, is often absolute. There are few data about the effects of such economic stress on children. It would be reasonable to assume that this is a particularly acute problem for teenagers, who are subject to peer pressure in relation to fashionable clothing and social expenditure; this may lead to them seeking paid work, possibly at the expense of long-term educational achievement, or to their obtaining financial reward from criminal activity.

Much has been written about the effects on children, particularly boys, of absent fathers, but it is difficult to disentangle the effects of the loss of a role model, the increased difficulties with the disciplining of boys experienced by single mothers and the socio-economic situation of single-parent families. Children in such families are significantly disadvantaged by their family circumstances.

During periods of their lives when their parents are single, children may experience a number of other adults as parental figures when their carers, usually mothers, seek another 'permanent' relationship. This may be particularly confusing for adolescents who would, at this age, often ignore the possibility of their parent's sexual activity and discover adult sexuality for themselves as an experience confirming their own separate identity.

Permanence of parenthood

Children regard their natural parents as permanent members of their families, whether or not they are separated from them by family breakdown, adoption, fostering or periods in institutional care; this is now reflected not only

87

in professional practice but in various laws and regulations. These include the Children Act (with its emphasis on continuing parental responsibility and the requirement for all services to make the needs of children paramount), the Criminal Justice Act, the Child Support Act and the Family Law Bill. Children come into a step family as a direct result of the loss of a parent either by death or divorce and need to establish relationships with at least one new family member who has not been a part of the child's picture of the family. Many children achieve this transition successfully, though it is widely believed that the possibility of a continuing relationship with both natural parents following divorce is a major advantage.

The effects of family breakdown

There is no dispute that the health and social costs of family breakdown are considerable for parents and their children. As well as the immediate economic costs discussed above, there is evidence that both parents are disadvantaged by the breakdown of their own relationship.

Mothers who care for the children face additional responsibilities for making decisions and managing discipline, as well as surviving on a smaller income and possibly needing to seek outside employment. One of the hypotheses suggested to explain the poor outcomes for children is that these are related, in part, to their mother's psychological health and ability to cope with the increased stresses and lack of personal support in single parenthood.

Following separation, fathers are also more likely to seek medical help. It has been suggested that in marriage men require and receive more personal reinforcement than vice versa, so that the loss of this relationship leaves men at risk of psychological disturbance associated with self-doubt and loss of role, particularly when they have not sought the end of the relationship. Fathers are unlikely to be granted residential responsibility for their children, even in circumstances where the woman has ended the marriage and is in employment while he is in a better position to offer full-time child care.

The disadvantage to children of family breakdown has been described in several research studies which have approached the problem from a variety of perspectives and methodologies.[1,2,3,4] Most recently a UK case/control study based on a population of school children showed that children experienced greater difficulties in reordered families and particularly those that had been reconstituted and then broken down again (one quarter of the sample).[4]

There is more consistency between these studies than variance. The picture that emerges is of many children experiencing an acute reaction to their parents' separation. This is evidenced in some by sadness, development of poor self-esteem and self-efficacy, psychosomatic and general health problems, behavioural disturbance, particularly in boys, difficulties with school performance and with peer and adult relationships. About three quarters of all referrals to child and adolescent psychiatry and psychology services are of children from reordered families. Since a maximum of twenty-five per cent of the relevant population are in this group this suggests an eight fold relative referral as compared to children in intact families. This figure is almost identical to the odds ratio (a statistical measure of probability) for referral to such services found in the Exeter Family Study.

These difficulties tend to reduce over time, particularly for girls in single-mother families and where parents are able to continue a relationship with each other which works sufficiently well for them to meet the needs of the child for easy, conflict-free contact with both parents. In spite of the abatement of these problems over time, children of parents who have separated have lowered long-term life chances. For example, on average they will finish full time education earlier, work in less skilled and less financially rewarding employment and develop close personal relationships earlier; if girls, they are more likely to have their first pregnancy in their teens. They are also likely to marry early and, if married, are more likely to become divorced.

Mechanisms of adverse effects on children

There is less consensus about the causal links between marital breakdown and the adverse outcomes for children. At one extreme are those who believe that nearly all the variance in outcomes is accounted for by family functioning, particularly the level of conflict or family violence that existed in the intact family before separation. A more generally accepted position would be that this is but one, though a major, associated factor. Other influences include the amount and content of post divorce conflict, access and contact arrangements for the child, socio-economic difficulties, the degree of disturbance to the child's daily life at the time of the separation, mother's psychological well-being and relationships with step parents.

Other issues for children

Children face a number of other challenges when their parents separate. While many children meet these successfully and in the process become more mature and self sufficient, many others are unable to overcome them. It is believed that parent's divorce is one of the important life events that may result in children's life trajectories altering towards greater risk of illness and disturbance. The problems children face include the likelihood of a period of economic deprivation, moving house and possibly neighbourhood and school, with the consequence that they lose contact with friends and have to settle into a new social environment. At home they are likely to have to come to terms with sharing the love and attention of their mother with her new partner and to have another life and life-style when on contact visits with their father, possibly in inappropriate accommodation.

Their father's parents are likely to reduce their contact with, and support of, the family, so that children may lose touch with their favourite grandparents. They may need to make new relationships with additional 'grandparents' and, more importantly, with step-brothers and sisters who might either be responsible for them or vice versa. Contact is a major source of friction for many divorced couples and the children may find themselves forced to go on visits they do not wish to make or may be prevented from seeing their non-resident parent as much, or as freely, as they would wish.

Causes of adverse outcomes for children

Interpretation of cause, as opposed to association, is fraught with difficulty, in common with much behavioural and sociological research, which in this case is complicated by the fact that individual researchers may be influenced by their own membership of 'super-intact' families or families that have experienced parental separation. There may be an unwillingness to acknowledge that parents who care deeply for the well-being of their children may have had to choose between a solution that would be of greatest benefit for their children and their family, as opposed to an alternative, which appears better for themselves as individuals. There is now agreement that the interests of children often conflict with those of separating or separated parents. An emphasis on the importance of keeping children's needs as a central consideration without their being 'caught in the middle' is fundamental to the proposed divorce law reform; this aim is clearly recognised in a statement by a group of six organisations particularly interested in families of all types.[5]

Conflict

It has long been known that conflict between parents, particularly when children are involved in the conflict, is associated with the development of problems for children whether in intact or reordered families. These problems are exhibited characteristically in boys by conduct disorders and in girls by evidence of internalised difficulties such as depression or eating disorders. Some studies have shown that the symptoms of childhood disequilibrium have their origins in the conflict experienced before marital breakdown and even suggest that the main cause of these disorders in children of divorced parents is exposure to conflict before separation.

Is a peaceful divorce better for children than continuing conflict?

The knowledge that conflict is damaging for children has been transmuted into an accepted wisdom that a peaceful divorce and an end to such conflict will be better for children than a continuing conflictual marriage. Such an hypothesis, for that is what it is, is not open to investigation because, in order to investigate it without unknown biases, it would be necessary to randomly divide families in conflict into two groups, one of which would be prevented from undergoing parental separation. Furthermore, it should be remembered that divorce does not always follow a marriage characterised by conflict. In many instances divorce follows a drifting apart of parents or a change in their relationship that results in the forming of new relationships by one or both partners outside their marriage. Commonly, in this situation, conflict is acute and associated with the events surrounding separation.

If it is accepted that many marriages will continue to end in irretrievable breakdown, even if the questions about the relative importance of various factors in relation to the outcome for children remain unanswered, a high priority must be to minimise these adverse effects for children.

Our children's inheritance

Many professionals working with children have serious concerns about the long-term well-being of the present generation of young adults and children. Some families find themselves no longer able to fulfil the vital functions of inculcating moral values or imposing restraints. To many, we appear to be introducing children to a society that has rejected a number of traditional values without identifying or espousing new codes to take their place. Some professionals, particularly those concerned with behaviourally and emotionally disturbed adolescent young men, would go further and suggest that we are sitting on a time bomb of anarchy.

Major changes in the world of work where jobs are no longer 'for life', but are essentially temporary, support notions of immediacy and impermanence. In such a climate of personal economic and political short-termism young people may find it difficult to enter marital relationships for life: 'for richer or for poorer, for better or for worse, in sickness or in health'. The evidence that many people are no longer able to maintain such long term commitments in circumstances where most areas of their lives are uncertain suggests an equally uncertain inheritance.

Ways forward

In examining what could or should be done to support families the following premise is suggested. For optimal development, intellectually, socially, morally and spiritually, children need to be nurtured and disciplined in an environment of love, provided by adults with whom they are able to establish long-term and safe relationships. This premise would have been accepted by most individuals at any time in the last two centuries. There is no evidence that these conditions can be provided other than in families. While some would suggest that it is possible, few of those engaged in vocations directly concerned with the welfare of children would consider it desirable. In spite of this there is little doubt that much social policy, politically correct thinking and actual political and economic regulation has, in proper attempts to support the most disadvantaged members of society, resulted in an increased emphasis on social parenting and a weakening of the role of the family.

At the same time the dramatic changes in the structure and permanence of families, discussed above, have radically altered the ease with which this environment might be achieved. We do not yet know whether a family that has the characteristics of family discussed in the early paragraphs of this chapter, but is not a nuclear family, can fulfil the same functions. What is clear is that it would be inappropriate simply to wait for the evidence. There is already a significant body of evidence that the present generation of children and young adults are experiencing adverse effects from the present situation, where those not nurtured in well-functioning nuclear families are disadvantaged. It is also clear that a substantial number of children cannot expect to look to their parents for permanent nurture as described above and that, for an increasing number of young people, the responsibility for this will to a greater extent fall on society.

Promotion of parenting

A first priority appears to be an avowal and promotion by society of the importance, value and status of child rearing and the family as an institution of value to society. For the foreseeable future child rearing is likely to remain a commitment of time made predominantly by women though the principle is not affected whether or not this is the case. Whatever the family arrangement there needs to be an acceptance of the importance of the roles of both parents. While women are able to raise children independently of men, the role of fathers may be particularly important for the social and moral development of boys. Men's roles as fathers may also be important in preventing the sidelining of men, particularly young men, as having no useful function in society.

The adverse effects of increased state involvement in social parenting have been recognised in other countries where similar changes have taken place, notably in the USA and Sweden. Both these countries, recognising that too much state support may disempower parents, have renewed emphasis on the roles of parents. In Sweden, a shift of social provision is hoped to facilitate partnership between state and parents with new employment and fiscal provisions that provide support for both parents to fulfil their family responsibilities. In other countries, such as France, there has been strong fiscal support for the role of families in health and education.

Fiscal policy could be radically altered to facilitate the promotion of parenting, without, necessarily, incurring enormous financial penalties. Some economists propose radical change, for example a basic income for every individual instead of benefits. The current arrangements are recognised to be 'anti-family' in some of their effects and are believed by many to be a disincentive for men to seek full-time employment. The problem of a large increase in the aged population coupled with a decrease in the work-force will only exacerbate these difficulties and place further strains on families.

Facilitating long-term parenting

The second area of concern that does appear to be amenable to intervention is the need to institute measures which will encourage parents to continue their role as parents throughout their lives, or at least until their children are independent. Divorce is now perceived by many as a right, and indeed the right of an adult not to have to live with an abusing partner is an important innovation of this century. Children also have rights. According to the UN Charter on the Rights of the Child, one of those rights is to be nurtured by two parents where possible and, where that is not possible, to be able to maintain meaningful, safe and conflict-free contact with both their natural parents.

During and after parental separation these rights very often conflict; it is then appropriate to re-examine rights in the light of possible duties. It is accepted in nearly all societies of the world that those who are the most vulnerable may expect others to undertake some responsibility for them; indeed in the case of children, who are more vulnerable than their parents, this is fundamental to the survival of humanity. If this responsibility is accepted, it is necessary to examine whether a parent's right to divorce has, in our society, become in some cases, a licence to seek greater personal fulfilment at the expense of their duty of care. We must accept that separation and divorce will continue to be commonplace, while hoping that the current trend towards increasingly temporary adult relationships can at least be halted. The continuing responsibility of parents to their children and the current failure of many parents to fulfil their duty of care has rightly been the focus of much thought, research, intervention and in 1996 a new Family Law Bill introduced by the Lord Chancellor.

The Family Law Bill 1996

The introductory paragraphs to this Bill, added during a stormy passage through the House of Lords, reaffirms the aim set out in the introduction to the preceding Green and White papers. It is that the legislation is intended to support the institution and permanence of marriage, in particular as the most appropriate family arrangement for the nurture of children. Many opponents of the Bill saw the removal of fault as a ground for divorce as under-mining the contractual basis of marriage. Those who opposed the Bill perceived that it would actually make divorce easier and quicker, further weakening the impor-tance and societal valuation of marriage. In contrast, sup-porters noted that (often unchallenged) fault-based facts were used as the mechanism to achieve 'quickie' divorce in a median time of six months for the three-quarters of all divorces that were 'fault' based. In addition to this major change in the ground for divorce, the Bill contains measures which aim to encourage parents to consider the option of reconciliation, ensures that they are given infor-mation about the possible adverse effects of divorce both for themselves and their children, precludes divorce for at least one year after the filing of papers (to allow time for reflection) and strongly supports mediation. This will be seen as the principal method of planning arrangements for the future care of children and the division of property and income. If there are children of the marriage their needs will be seen as paramount in decisions that are made.

Family mediation

Divorce mediation has been thought by many researchers and jurisdictions in other parts of the world to be an important mechanism to reduce parental conflict. It is designed to enable parents to negotiate with each other reasonably, but fairly, and usually to have their agreement checked by their own lawyer. This has been available for many years, free of charge to couples in contested proceedings concerning children in the private law sphere (from the Court Welfare Service), but otherwise only privately (e.g. from the Family Mediators Association), or as a combination of charitable service and client contribution (e.g. from National Family Mediation and Family Mediation Scotland). Under the new arrangements of the Family Law Bill, mediation will be available to all parents and will be eligible for legal aid. The Lord Chancellor's Department is commissioning evaluated pilot initiatives to establish the most appropriate and efficacious models of provision.

Few of the services provided by the latter organisations currently have arrangements to ensure that the voice of children is clearly heard, for example by allowing them to participate in the mediation process, but bearing in mind their susceptibility to adult pressure. Giving the child a voice in arrangements which will directly affect their lives is entirely consistent with the current emphasis on the rights of children to have their views taken into account, as in the UN Charter on The Rights of the Child and embodied in The Children Act 1989. It is important to ensure that in this process the child is not made to feel any responsibility for the outcome.

Other countries, notably Australia and New Zealand, are perceived as being ahead in these matters. The existence of separate Family Courts with less formal proceedings is seen as important in facilitating a whole family approach and giving a different perception of the force and role of the law in relation to family issues. In this country the Children Act does include many of the elements seen as desirable in meeting the needs of children but many of its provisions (such as the appointment of guardians ad litem) are generally only applicable in the Public Law. There is a view that a radical review and reorganisation of the family justice system is necessary.

Addressing the increase in divorce

There is some concern that mediation will not adequately deal with situations where there is domestic violence and special arrangements are in place to address such problems. Divorce is infrequently sought because of violence, whether physical or psychological, though its prevalence is unestimated. A larger number of parents separate because one or other is not fulfilling their commitments to the other's satisfaction. There is also evidence that after divorce many adults regret their decision which has in the meantime exposed their children to a significant risk of reduced life chances.[6]

In such circumstances it is reasonable to ask whether anything could be done to reduce the number of parents becoming separated and divorced. The role of a marriage contract in facilitating permanent personal commitment is uncertain, but it is likely that an even greater proportion of child-bearing cohabitations end in separation than do marriages; it is known that marriages preceded by cohabitation (with the same partner) are more likely to end in divorce. Cohabitation is sometimes adopted by couples who are uncertain as to their long-term commitment to each other as well as by others as a prelude to a marriage or permanent relationship. The Child Support Act emphasises the contractual and enduring nature of parenting. It might have been seen as a pro-family measure had it been introduced with greater adroitness and seen less as a fiscal measure to reduce expenditure on benefits, had fewer areas of its application been open to criticism and demonstrated a more successful transfer of family income to separated single parents.

Education is a key area

While health and social services and economic changes have all facilitated 'social' parenting there has been no attempt by educationalists to take over the roles of parents. In contrast to the perceived priorities of education in the eighteenth and nineteenth centuries, many members of the teaching profession have not seen it as appropriate for schools to attempt to influence belief or behaviour. Such attitudes have been reinforced by conflicts of cultural practice, particularly of religious belief, that are thrown into sharp relief in our multi-cultural society. It is widely accepted that our present education system is almost entirely focused towards academic and vocational learning and has very little investment in what might be termed 'education for life'.

In recent decades many influential academics believed it was beyond their remit to seek to influence values or behaviour, such as reducing early and medically disadvantageous sexual activity. Rather it has been suggested that education should be solely concerned with the giving of information and the teaching of skills needed to evaluate facts for themselves. The latter task is however an extremely ambitious educational aim and may not be achievable. It would require investment in highly sophisticated educational techniques such as those embodied in social learning and associated theories.

Such practice also ignores the effect of the media which have not demonstrated the same qualms about undue influence and the often malign effects of peer pressure. The result is that children and adolescents are presented with widely divergent perspectives of behaviour but may have insufficient skills, maturity or moral guidance to weigh and evaluate difficult choices appropriately.

There are in fact many more areas of agreement than disagreement in our society as to what constitute appropriate and acceptable values and behaviour. Much could be done to address these issues within a solid consensus. Where there is disagreement, education in school can be used to teach children how to evaluate different arguments and, perhaps most importantly, how to negotiate and accept compromise, recognising that in many areas there is no single answer.

On a practical level, the education that we provide to assist young people in this area can only be described as lamentable. We teach few skills to assist them to manage what are, possibly, the most critical and problematic areas of their transition to adulthood, their sexuality and the developing and maintaining of adult relationships. Little, if anything, is taught about the meaning of love or the consideration of duties to each other and children within marriage. There is little undergraduate training of teachers to perform these tasks as a vocation, little incentive for the study of such matters in the National Curriculum, little examination of the many areas that would be amenable to assessment and often little credit for teachers or students who devote time to them. This curriculum must be accommodated in schools as part of an enormous and, perhaps unattainable, list of subjects to be covered within the cross-curricular teaching of personal, social and moral education, for which teachers themselves have usually received only limited short- course or study-day learning opportunities.

It should be no surprise that in spite of public concern about this area of education it is, in practice, often marginalised in our schools and colleges. This situation must be addressed at a time when preparation for parenthood may be more critical than it has ever been before.

In addition to reforms of the ways in which divorce in this country is conducted, a radical reappraisal of the school curriculum should be carried out. This should refocus, at least a major part of the syllabus, away from academic skills and training for employment, which a growing number of people will only achieve for a relatively short spell of their lives, and towards the skills for living that are apparently at a greater deficit in our society than ever before in recent centuries.

Conclusions

The rapidity of social change in the structures of the family in Britain has undoubtedly placed many of its vital functions for the continuation of our society in jeopardy. Many of the results of social, economic and political influence on the family were unforeseen. The possibility that these changes could be reversed by planned intervention must therefore be open to serious question. There is, in any case, little evidence that there is any general wish to turn the clock back. It is, however, possible to plan interventions aimed at minimising the unwanted effects of the impact of these changes on the functioning of families by political and professional evolution of the economy, the law and of education and other services. When social change threatens social order there is a need to identify innovative ways to preserve what is considered to be of value while allowing change in that which is undesirable. In the context of the family the challenge is to develop supports for families who face extraordinarily complex tasks in our society. Some suggested priorities for this process have been presented.

A personal note

Readers who know me may be puzzled by the lack of reference to Christian belief and absolutes, such as truth, in this chapter. However, I believe I am intellectually most able to defend my belief in God, both to myself and others, by arguments that I would present as an apologist. The fact that the principles enumerated in the New Testament are profound, have been robust over time and appear to work well in many different cultures of the world provides an apologetic argument for their origin from beyond human experience. On the other hand, I believe it is inappropriate to suggest that Christian doctrine should be the sole criterion for the development of policy in our post-Christian, multi-faith society. Nonetheless, readers may care to compare and contrast the situation in which we find ourselves at the end of the twentieth century with that which they would predict might have pertained had the social enlightenment of this century been characterised by a reinterpretation, rather than an almost complete abandonment, of Christian belief.

Notes

1. Wallerstein J, Kelly J. *Surviving the Breakup: How Children and Parents Cope with Divorce*. London: Grant McIntyre, 1980.
2. Wadsworth MEJ. *The Imprint of Time: Childhood, History and Adult Life*. Oxford: Clarendon Press, 1991.
3. Hetherington EM. *Family Relations Six Years after Divorce. In: Remarriage and Step-parenting Today: Research and Theory* (Parsley K, Ihinger-Tallman M eds). New York: Smedford Press, 1987.
4. Cockett M, Tripp JH. *The Exeter Family Study.* Exeter University Press, 1994.
5. *Beyond the Year of the Family: Defining the Agenda.* London:

King George VI and Queen Elizabeth Foundation of St Catherine's, 1995. ISSN 0955–3517.

6. McAllister F, Dominion J, Mansfield P, Breen S, Morrod J, Percival J (eds). *Marital Breakdown and the Health of the Nation*. London: One Plus One, 1995.

CHAPTER SEVEN

THE PERSONAL MONEY MANAGEMENT CRISIS

Alasdair Barron

Alasdair Barron was formerly Director of Credit Action, Cambridge which campaigned against the impact of credit and debt on personal, family and national life.

Although personal debt has always been a problem for some, its growth from the early 1980s constitutes a new phenomenon. The number of people in financial difficulties and the extent of their indebtedness quickly reached crisis proportions. The reasons for this, the consequences including the response by lenders and borrowers, and the possible solutions are discussed in this chapter.

Definitions

To understand personal debt it is necessary to briefly define terms. 'Consumer debt' is taken to mean unsecured debt. Typically this would be credit card debt, a store account, or other borrowing where no asset of the borrowers was secured as collateral if they were unable to repay. This is separate from mortgage or other debts secured on property or other assets.

Broadly speaking, personal debt can occur in two ways. Poverty debt is characterised by a lack of assets and is associated with the usual poverty indicators including low income and relatively small commitments, which even so, are greater than income. Accommodation would probably be rented. Overcommitment debt is where there are significant assets, including perhaps a house with a mortgage, but for whatever reason commitments exceed assets.

Factors in indebtedness

A number of factors have led to increased indebtedness. Simply stated these include the management of the economy, unemployment, the availability, amount and promotion of loans and financial services, and the reduction of social security support. Simultaneously society has increasingly become more materialistic, and traditional restraints against borrowing have decreased.

The growth of the economy during the first ten years after the Conservative Party came to power in 1979 created a house purchase boom. Home ownership was seen as desirable, and was strongly endorsed by the Government and the powerful voice of Mrs Thatcher herself. As the economy was expanding, unemployment low (at least in the early 1980s), and house purchase desirable, many saw this as their time of opportunity and borrowed to purchase their way onto the housing ladder. The programme of council house selling further increased the number of dwellings in private ownership.

At the same time, mortgage lending criteria were being relaxed to such a degree that the risk to the borrower was becoming unacceptably high. Interest rate rises caused by the Bank of England raising the bank rate affected lenders who then raised their mortgage borrowing interest rates accordingly. Hence, mortgage repayment amounts reached levels which would have been unimaginable a few years earlier. The house market slowed, and the term 'negative equity' was heard for the first time in a lifetime.

Growth of consumer debt

The growth of consumer debt has been particularly striking. In 1975, consumer debt amounted to less than £5 billion. By 1984 it had exceeded £15 billion, and reached £50.6 billion in 1990. In addition, the interest rates charged tend to be much higher than for secured credit, enhancing the effect of even small levels of consumer borrowing. The importance of consumer debt is that it now competes for a significant share of the household budget—and when interest rates go up its demands need to be serviced as well as those of mortgage debt and normal living expenses. Further comprehensive financial information on credit and debt is given in a report prepared for the Movement for Christian Democracy.[1]

Unemployment

Employment, or the lack of it, is the equivalent of day and night for most people. The loss of a job, seen in the early 1980s predominantly as a thinning down of labour intensive industries, and then later increasingly affecting management grades, is still a possibility. For example, the privatised sector comprising telecommunications, gas, electricity and water are expected to shed a total of 250,000 employees, the size of the population of the city of Stoke, by the year 2000.[2]

Social security hardship one-off payments (crisis grants) were replaced by loans.

Bank lending

The promotion of credit aided the expansion of lending by making borrowing more attractive. The big banks, suffering from unprofitable lending elsewhere, targeted the British consumer market, and worked to increase their share of consumer and mortgage lending. The battle intensified as young people, who the banks and building societies hoped would become first-time accounts, received increasing attention in order to capture new business. The abolition of cross-border trading within the EC on 1 January 1992 further concentrated the lenders' minds.

Student loans

A process of cutting student grants began with grants being frozen in 1990, and continued with 10% reductions for each of three years starting in 1994. This is a shift in government policy from full funding for education and requires students to take loans. In terms of number, 180,000 (28%) students had loans in 1990/91 rising to about 430,000 (47%) in 1993/94. Student loan lending increased from £70 million in 1990/91 to £317 million in 1993/94. At that time, over 20% had considered dropping out due to financial pressure. Around 50% of students had part-time jobs during term, and of those, half had missed studies, and three-quarters felt their work was adversely affected.[3]

Impact of debt

The impact on people was described in *Families in Debt*,[4] which was possibly the first report to chronicle the national realities of personal debt. In a survey of over 1,000 people with multiple debt problems in 1987, the average amount of debt was £4,500 per person, and the average number of debts over six.

Four years later, debt counsellors indicated that the average amount owed by clients in their debt counselling practices had risen to around £10,000, and the average number of debts was around 10. The three most important debts in rank order were to:

(a) finance companies
(b) banks
(c) credit card companies.

Eighty per cent of the survey sample were less than forty-six years old. The time needed to repay debt, on the most optimistic assumptions, was more than nine years on average, eighteen years for those on disposable incomes of less than £100 per week, and thirty years for the unemployed.

In-depth interviews indicated the reasons for debt, in rank order:

(a) sudden reduction in income
(b) unexpected increase in needs
(c) overspending
(d) emotional crises.

In general the impact of debt on the health of individuals and families was severe, exacerbating current problems in the household to an alarming degree. These included depression, anxiety, social withdrawal and sometimes domestic violence. Occasionally suicide resulted. An assessment by the NSPCC also indicated that debt was a strongly associated factor in child abuse. County court summonses for default rose rapidly, from 535,000 in 1951, to 2,358,000 in 1989, to peak at 3,388,000 in 1991. The 1995 level is roughly compatible to the 1989 level.

The situation whereby a mortgage on a family home was used to finance a small business start-up was a frequent cause of concern, particularly as the small business failure rate rose. If the business was not doing well, the family home was potentially under threat and a source of worry, particularly for the wife, who saw the possibility of the family not having a roof over their heads.

The rise in mortgage default increased steeply, as did the three month in arrears figures. These arrears figures indicated the likely future default picture, and were watched closely as an indicator of difficulties ahead.

Response to debt

The personal response to increasing debt problems is to work towards at least matching income and expenditure, by maximising income and controlling expenditure.

Lenders were often concerned that leniency on debt repayments would lead to them being taken advantage of, and then on to the encouragement of irresponsible borrowing. This is an understandable fear, for a small percentage of people would undoubtedly take such advantage. However, probably over ninety per cent of the population are concerned to pay their debts, and not to be able to do so causes them tremendous stress.

What lenders never did properly was to take adequate account of the borrower's overall commitment picture. Loan applications were processed without adequate reference to other commitments, and often without face-to-face validation. There were at least two reasons for this. First, the opposition by marketing managers to requests for financial information—which they regard as a 'turn-off'. Secondly, the extra administration costs and time involved.

For small loans, with the current volume of business it would be impossible to make substantial checks. However, key factors such as the number of loans possessed by an individual and a realistic assessment of repayment rate still needs to be made. In the case of mortgages, though, it is hard to see why this, probably the primary loan which any individual is likely to take out, is the subject of an interview in perhaps less than fifty per cent of mortgage applications.

The Office of Fair Trading (OFT) has made a major contribution to equitable lending practices. A series of popular booklets was published in quantity and promoted vigorously, even to the extent of organising a popular phone-in on two BBC radio channels where calls were answered by teams of debt counsellors. The OFT's role in working for transparency and clarity in lending transactions resulted in health warnings on advertisements and required the display of Annual Percentage Rates (APRs). It also performs another vital function, the operation of a licensing system for credit granters.

In the USA, the lending rule of thumb is that expenditure on loan servicing should not exceed thirty per cent of personal income. With tax at say twenty per cent of income, and utilities at say fifteen per cent, a reasonable amount remains for food and other necessary expenses. On the basis of the lack of information existing on the totality of an individual's borrowing commitments mentioned above, UK lenders would not know the position of their client clearly enough in order to observe this or any other lending guide-line. Responsible lending and borrowing are two sides of the same coin. In the same way that a borrower should not try to borrow more than they can repay, the lender should avoid lending an applicant into trouble.

Mortgage lending

The relaxation in mortgage lending deserves special mention, because it added fuel to the housing boom, and when that bubble burst, borrowers' commitments were the greater. Traditional mortgage lending was based on a 2 x the primary annual salary, sometimes with an allowance for a second income. In the late 1980s, this slid up to 4 x salary, coupled with generous allowances for a second income. The service load alone becomes very heavy. If the borrower runs into financial difficulties then servicing the loan rapidly becomes unsustainable. It is immediately evident that lending on the above terms exceeds the USA rule of thumb given above.

Probably the most significant reason why this happened was because the 'level playing field' tilted. In the absence of agreed industry lending standards, people would take their business to the highest lender, in order to purchase the best property they could afford. It quickly became impossible for conservative lenders to maintain a traditional lending position as custom would go elsewhere.

Consumer credit

In the case of consumer credit, the Consumer Credit Act 1974 said that 'unreasonable' interest rates may not be charged, but it nowhere defined what they were. To take a simple example, interest of, say, thirty per cent per week grosses up to hundreds of thousands of per cent over a year. Admittedly rates of those levels were applicable often to small loans, but when part of a small income they were penal.

It was always an objective of mine to see a ruling for unreasonable interest pursued in the courts in order to establish a precedent of sorts, albeit at a low level. The difficulties experienced in doing this were that people were fearful to take a case to court, and meeting the financial cost of such an action. The loss of a case of loan sharking in Strathclyde, on a technicality, which resulted in the victim having to leave Scotland, is both a tragedy and an unpleasant reminder of reality.

Financial stability

The process of helping those in debt to regain financial stability is well known, and has been described in detail.[5,6] Basically, a budget is prepared listing income and expenditure, and debts are divided into priority and non-priority debts. In order to live, basic living expenses are deducted from available income, then priority debts are serviced. Any remaining money is used to pay non-priority debts.

The financial statement is used to request extended payment terms if needed for priority debts, and also to negotiate repayment terms with creditors in the case of non-priority debts.

Usually non-priority creditors are offered a pro rata amount that the debtor can afford to pay to all creditors. As each creditor receives the same pro rata amount, they normally accept. It is usually important though, to have the help of a debt counsellor (now money advisor) since companies are more likely to accept the client's position if a professional has been involved in the case preparation. A key factor in the 'sorting-out process' is communication. Nothing causes more aggravation than if a creditor gets no response to their communications. Worried borrowers who can't pay make the situation worse by delaying, when in fact early contact facilitates the finding of a solution.

Debt counselling throws up some amazing contrasts. The comment made to me that 'I'm in debt, but I take two foreign holidays a year—I love the sun' is an indication of the way some people live with incipient problems. Older people may feel that, having saved all their lives for little luxuries, that young people in debt get off too lightly.

The finance industry responded to growing debt problems by launching the Money Advice Trust, after a lengthy enquiry chaired by Lord Ezra. The assets come from contributions from the banking, building society and insurance industries. The Trust gave seven grants in 1992, totalling £173,000.

The increasing availability of credit was coupled with a massive growth in credit cards, in 1990 30 million in the UK, compared to 8 million in France, and 2 million in Germany. This is a concern since while the disciplined user may well have avoided charges by paying within a limited 'interest free' time period, many others ended up paying.

The growth of credit reference agencies, to perhaps five national groups was rapid. Building from voter registration records, they added information from lenders on defaults, and this could be accessed on several levels of detail depending on subscription level by a credit granter who wanted information on an applicant.

The idea of credit unions has been a minor but consistent theme. Adherents believe they formalise self-help within a constructive community context, which they do. They help savers to save consistently, and to borrow mainly small amounts advantageously, after a minimum period of membership has elapsed. I believe that in the right circumstances credit unions can have a unique and strongly positive contribution to make. Where they seem to work best is where the association between members, for example within a professional group or location is strong. However, in view of the low rate of return, most people would rather put their money in a local bank or building society branch where the return is higher.

The biblical view of wealth

It has been estimated that one in every six verses in the New Testament is on money, wealth or poverty. And in the Old Testament, money, wealth and poverty are the second most important issues next to idolatry.[7] The most important issue is the idolatry of money and material things over God. There is the stern warning that the *love* of money is the root of all evil.[8] Even this simple concept does not seem to be widely understood—I was once introduced to a meeting as the speaker who was going to talk on 'money which is the root of all evil'. Few people would say that they love money more than God! Yet in practice many have clung to their money.

In terms of personal attitude to money, the Christian position on wealth, generosity and living simply is developed in *Families in Debt.*[4] Three biblical principles were identified as being of central importance. These were the principles of justice, mercy and hope.

The principle of justice obligated the borrower to repay (i.e. not to steal), and if unable to pay then to enter indentured labour for a period. The lender was required to meet three obligations. First, certain minimum rights of the debtor with respect to collateral. Secondly, to wipe out debts every seventh year, and thirdly, not to refuse to lend to the poor when to do so might mean loss when the year of debt release arrived. Application of the justice principle today has been developed further[4] to give a range of measures which would lead to respect of the borrower in a situation where the balance of power is greatly in favour of the lender.

The principle of mercy, which covers all moral obligations, by definition covers financial transactions as well. Is it merciful to advertise goods to those on low incomes who realistically will not be able to buy them? Mercy could also be expressed by companies generously supporting money advice to help those in debt, and by a more generous attitude to debt write-off when borrowers are in real difficulties.

The principle of hope, which the year of debt release built into the Old Testament system, limited the period of debt and gave more hope to debtors. Many of those in debt today find hope lacking, as their debt pay-off periods are measured in years, sometimes very many years. What happens instead, is a lengthy period of anxious wrangling which sometimes results in the debtor being taken through the judicial process with the associated anxiety. Eventually the debtor pays some or all of the amount or the lender writes it off. In general terms though, court processes have become simpler and more favourable with various representational and simplification reforms.

The issue of interest is challenging. The Old Testament,

which Jesus endorsed, is clear that interest was not to be received from fellow Israelites and the Church followed this principle until the time of the reformer Calvin. The Roman Catholic Church continued to oppose interest until 1854. But is the biblical position of 'zero interest' the correct one? Even though the question is somewhat hypothetical because it would be impossible to return to a zero interest position easily, is that the right target?

Perhaps the main effect of 'zero interest' was to give money the role of a kind of 'social glue'. For example, if money was required for business development or indeed any other purpose, under this scenario it would have to come from relatives. And that would mean their involvement in the use of that money from start to finish of the loan, providing advice and support whether the borrower liked it or not. Currently borrowing only has to satisfy the lender's requirements, and is independent of family relationships.

The Christian position on generosity is also challenging. It encourages a heartfelt response to God's love, but in practice, while the principle is acknowledged it could be acted on much more emphatically. Perhaps this is because of fear—fear that we will be duped, or that the money will not be used wisely, or achieve the desired effect, or even that the giver will not have enough left if they give. But Christians are assured[9] not only that they will be blessed in giving, but also that they will always have enough—an amazing promise. What more encouragement to giving could there be?

Responding to the money management crisis

The need for money advice in the late 1980s reached impossible proportions. The Citizen's Advice Bureau (CAB), who provided, and even now continue to provide the vast proportion of money advice, was overtaken by a tidal wave of requests numbering up to 500,000 per year. It was estimated at one point that there was a ninety-six per cent shortfall in advice provision.

Credit Action, a money management charity, carried out a number of campaigning initiatives but was not able to secure sufficient funds to campaign effectively in the long term and so turned its attention to awareness raising and education. Some examples of campaigning issues follow.

A levy on lenders was proposed to generate funds to pay for much needed money advice. It was proposed that a fraction of a percent of loans would be collected and put into a fund, and those funds spent on training staff and enhancing facilities. The campaign raised the issue in Parliament through Early Day Motions achieving considerable cross party support.

Some lobbying effort was put into trying to achieve fairer terms for cash purchasers, which would have helped poorer people who mainly pay by cash for food and essentials. In effect credit card purchasers get a discount because retailers pay the card companies about 1.5% of the price of the goods. It was felt that this charge should be borne only by card users, and the price reduced to cash purchasers.

Most people want to pay off their debts, but on small disposable incomes that is difficult. So Credit Action proposed an 'earnings disregard'[10] which would have allowed some earnings to go directly to debt repayment, while any social security payments were maintained. For example, if someone in debt took an extra job in an effort to earn to pay off debt, this would be allowed to happen without affecting benefits. Unfortunately the official view was that social security had first call on all earnings, and of course the more earnings the less benefit would be payable.

Education

The need for money management training and teaching materials was not met by existing materials in the early

1990s. In broad terms, published literature for adults tended to deal with budgeting and tax returns from a middle-class perspective, and had insufficient coverage of personal debt and what could be done if you found yourself in that situation. The need for a training package for Church members was identified and *Mind Over Money* was produced by Credit Action to meet that need. The fear that 'credit was too easily available' was a widespread concern.

For schools, while commercial product leaflets were available, there was almost no satisfactory teaching material. Coursework was needed which covered the range of issues important to students in a rounded and unbiased way. In an innovative project funded by the National Westminster Bank, Credit Action produced *Your Money Matters*, a video teaching pack for fourteen to sixteen year olds. In three lessons it dealt with budgeting, money services and saving, and credit and debt. The use of role plays and techniques such as grouping students in pairs to calculate their income and expenditure generated strong student involvement. The pack, which cost over £30 a copy, sold into a third of secondary schools in two years.

The challenge now is to develop and deliver relevant material to other age groups, perhaps across the age range from primary to 'A' level, so that sound money management thinking becomes part of the curriculum long term, and eventually a subject in its own right at GCSE level.

Values, which were only touched on in *Your Money Matters* under the heading of 'needs' and 'wants', have in my view a much wider and largely unrecognised relevance. If young people do not have a strong moral basis for decisions, then when the heat is turned up, confusion and perhaps violence is likely to result.

I visited the Watts suburb of Los Angeles in 1992 to see the situation after the riots first hand, and to look at educational provision. Two years later, the L.A. United School District had 'only an 83.4% attendance rate in its high schools'. There were wider problems too. 'Every eight seconds of the school day, an American student drops out of school. Every sixty-seven seconds, a teenager has a baby. Every seven minutes a child is arrested for a drugs-related offence. Every year the American school system graduates 700,000 young people who cannot read their diplomas. This is the story of a nation at risk.'[11] If a moral education is not provided in the UK it will be our story too.

Helping personally

The potential for constructive action is tremendous. For example, by utilising abilities which already exist within a local community. Those with financial skills could make them available to people who want to start the process of taking action to get out of debt. Incidentally, being willing to ask for help in solving a debt problem is extremely difficult for many people, who often get into serious debt step by step until they are finally forced to seek assistance.

People who want to help by giving their time could consider working with their local CAB. As part of a national organisation with the resources to answer difficult debt questions, the CAB may be willing to offer money advice training in return for a certain number of volunteer hours during the week.

One way of helping financially is to put money into local trusts (or even form a new trust) to relieve debt directly or make the lives of those in difficulty easier by meeting needs such as educational expenses. The trustees then shoulder the responsibility of making the funding allocation decisions.

The future

Better understanding of personal financial issues brought about by money management education, government legislation, clearer literature, and the support of the media is likely to mean that people manage their money better in future.

However, there are major factors over which people have little control. For example, the bank rate largely determines the cost of consumer credit and mortgages, and corporate decisions may result in redundancy. The loss of a job will continue to be the major cause of severe indebtedness for many people. In addition, fading moral values will cause more problems, because the will to meet obligations by being truthful, honest and responsible is decreasing.

The moral context of money management (which is often taken for granted), is a vital area and one where Christian values have much to offer. Whether it is in our own attitude to money and its use, the challenge to give generously, or the need to work continually towards just and fair economic systems, the Bible offers a revolutionary challenge which is largely ignored today and needs to be rediscovered.

Notes

1. Jubilee Policy Group. *Escaping the Debt Trap, the Problem of Consumer Credit and Debt in Britain Today.* Cambridge: Jubilee Centre, 1991.
2. *The Guardian*, August 6th, 1994.
3. Sources: Student Loans Company, the NUS and Credit Action.
4. Jubilee Centre. *Families in Debt.* Cambridge: Jubilee Centre, 1988. Research Paper No. 7
5. Schluter M, Lee D. *Credit and Debt: Sorting it out.* London: Marshall Pickering, 1989.
6. Tondeur K. *Escape from Debt.* Cambridge: Credit Action, 1993.
7. Matthew 6:19–24.
8. 1 Timothy 6:10.
9. 2 Corinthians 9:6–8.

10. Williams B. *Cleaning up the Debt Environment.* Cambridge: Jubilee Centre Publications, 1990. p 37.
11. Associated Examining Board. Business Matters No 9. 1994. ISSN 0968–2015.

CHAPTER EIGHT

THE IMPACT OF GAMBLING
AND THE NATIONAL LOTTERY

Keith Tondeur

Keith Tondeur is Director of Credit Action, Cambridge and previously spent twenty-two years in stockbroking. He has written several books on money management and on the impact of the lottery and of credit and debt on personal, family and national life.

> The whore and gambler, by the state
> licensed, build the nation's fate.[1]

The Lottery, with its weekly payout of enormous prizes was the one public event to which the proles paid serious attention. It was probable that there were some millions of proles for whom the Lottery was their principal, if not the only reason, for staying alive. It was their delight, their folly, their anodyne, their intellectual stimulant. Where the Lottery was concerned even people who could barely read and write seemed capable of intricate calculations and staggering feats of memory. There was a whole tribe of men who made a living simply by selling systems forecasts and lucky amulets.[2]

People looking back in twenty-five years' time may find that this was the release of a great evil in society. A quarter or half a million extra compulsive gamblers could mean a huge amount of misery.[3]

Ever since the launch of the National Lottery in 1994, the

nation appears to have been swept along by gambling fever. If you have walked along your high street in recent months at around eight o'clock on a Saturday evening you may have felt that everything was remarkably quiet. This could be because people are 'glued' to their television sets waiting for the weekly National Lottery numbers to be drawn. For many it has become an obsession—an increasingly desperate attempt to find happiness by fantasising about the delights that riches would bring. It has been calculated that over ninety per cent of the adult population has bought at least one lottery ticket and that fifty-eight per cent buy them every week. It is easy to see how this becomes an obsession. You pick six numbers but on the first Saturday they don't come up. Disappointment follows and maybe you think you'll give it a miss next week. Then fear can so easily take over. What happens if you don't buy a ticket next week and then the same numbers do come up—won't you be kicking yourself for the rest of your life? So you do it week after week. Yet the likelihood of winning anything significant is extremely remote.

There's nothing wrong . . . .

Surely there's nothing wrong with buying the odd ticket here and there? What harm can it do? Sadly, the answer is that it can do quite a lot of harm. At Credit Action we have had calls on our helpline from people who are suffering the consequences. One lady told how she had bought clothes for her children from a catalogue and had got into debt because her husband had been spending the repayment money on lottery tickets. Another case shows the danger of the instant scratch cards. A man was at the airport waiting to board his flight. While he was waiting he went into a newsagents and bought some scratch cards. When he found he hadn't won anything he bought more and more. Even when he won small amounts he used the cash to buy more cards. Eventually he completely cleared the shop of instant cards. Even allowing for the small sums he had won he had spent £490 on nothing.

Living for the Lottery

But very real tragedies also occur. This was highlighted recently in the national press which carried the very sad news of a fifty-one-year-old man who had killed himself directly as a result of the National Lottery. He regularly bought a batch of tickets and each week he entered the same numbers. One Sunday he came to check his tickets which he had thought were valid until that week but he found they had expired the week before. He then realised that he had had all the winning numbers and he had lost his family and a friend a million pounds each. In shock he went upstairs and shot himself in the head.

A police source said, 'The man had obviously flipped. He was a church-goer and a very fine man with no dark side to his character. You can never judge what people are capable of at times of stress.' A neighbour said, ' He was the nicest man in our street. He worked for the church and was always visiting the sick.' However, perhaps the most enlightening comments came from the man's newsagent from whom he bought the lottery tickets, He said, 'The National Lottery does strange things to people. They become obsessed. For some of my customers it is all they seem to live for. They spend their last pennies on it each week. It is very sad that these are the extremes gambling can lead to.'

A nation of gamblers

Gamblers Anonymous is already voicing 'great concern' at the number of people who are getting hooked on the Lottery and the purchase of instant or 'scratch' cards. They are seeing children as young as ten getting hooked on scratch cards. About £100 million is spent on lottery tickets each week with another £50 million going on the various 'instant' cards. In fact the sums spent on the Lottery are now so large that they were recently cited as a major source of growth in the national economy! When you add the tens of millions more which are gambled on the pools, horses, dogs and even bingo, I think it becomes clear that we have become a nation of gamblers.

I believe there are very mixed views on the National Lottery. At first, apart from a few 'killjoy' churchmen and moralists, very few saw much, if any, harm in it. Nowadays barely a day goes past without some article praising or criticising aspects of the National Lottery. The initial critics, many opposed to gambling per se, have been joined by others concerned at the regulator's role, the latest winner's reaction or, more generally, the fear of growing addiction. Everyone now appears to have an opinion on the merits or otherwise of the National Lottery.

Potential benefits of the Lottery

I think it might be helpful at this point to list some of the benefits the National Lottery has brought.

The beneficial impact of giving to charities and the arts

It is important to recognise that while some charities have suffered as a result of the National Lottery many others have received funding that they would otherwise have struggled to obtain. My own personal view is that much of the criticism has been 'self'-motivated—either 'it's not fair we are suffering' or 'you're not picking the right charities, i.e. the ones that I like'.

The planning required by charities before applying for funds

I believe that the National Lottery Charities Board is quite stringent in reviewing applications to it and consequently any requests for funding have to be worked out very carefully. I believe this professional approach will actually help a considerable number of charities to define accurately their priorities and ambitions and, ultimately, their ability to achieve them. Lucy Pratt of the Scottish Council for Voluntary Organisations agrees: 'It's put a rocket up behind some charities who have been quite complacent in the past about always being able to raise money.'

The bonding of syndicates

Many family groups or syndicates at work have got together to buy lottery tickets. This undoubtedly increases camaraderie and can boost a feeling of team spirit. Incidentally, the danger of a syndicate winning the jackpot and deciding en bloc to leave work is now so strong that businesses can buy insurance to protect them should that happen! Ten per cent of players are known to play the on-line game in a group. Others have office sweepstakes on the number of the bonus ball with fifty tickets being sold and the winner scooping the pool. Smaller office syndicates even gamble on which star sign Mystic Meg will mention first—now that is a conversation-stopper!

Fun, anticipation and dreams

I am sure that the reason most people enjoy doing the Lottery is because it gives them a chance to dream. It is a dream of release from reality—a dream of sunshine, sand, leisure and the ability to give two fingers to the boss, the mortgage, the debts and the desperate attempts to 'keep up with the Jones's. In your dream they have no chance of catching up with you! But you can also dream of being able to do good things for your family and friends so that people can see your true nature. For many too it is 'harmless fun'. Just £1 or so a week and a quietly hopeful wait for Saturday night.

Is the Lottery harmful?

But one has to ask, just because most people are unharmed by it does that make it right? What message does it give to society? The slave trade didn't directly harm or affect most people in Britain at the time but it said something about that society and it certainly didn't make it right. The lottery is popular but then so were public hangings and they weren't right. On reflection, I do believe the balance needed between the rights and responsibilities of an individual and society have moved much too far into the 'right's' position. At the moment we all tend to fight our corner to justify our position and find it almost impossible to say sorry and take the blame ourselves. It is my 'right'. The 'responsibility' is always somebody else's.

This Government and the media have given the National Lottery unprecedented support and publicity. So on one level it is a shared national experience, a bit of fun for millions, but its long-term implications and what it says about our society is frightening. We are in a pervasive gambling environment and as such up to eighty-six per cent of adults will gamble. Our experience of the Lottery has mirrored that in New Jersey where the results exceeded all but the most wildly optimistic predictions and demonstrated what a well-designed and aggressively merchandised Lottery could produce. So it is that a 'get rich quick' attitude has entered all aspects of our everyday life and it is likely to spread and spread with incalculable effects. In the nineties we have felt totally insecure, stressed out and uncomfortable and thus we are desperate for escape. So if our desires are to be frustrated by society perhaps Mystic Meg will come and lift us out of our sad existence.

Promotion of the Lottery

Gambling in Britain has been growing, even excluding the National Lottery. In the last five years the number of fruit

machines has increased by over 50,000 to 2,570,000. Their
£3 maximum pay-out was increased to £10 recently. Even
before this was done the average profit per machine was
£14 per week. Until the National Lottery the Government
had always controlled the promotion of opportunities to
gamble, although there has been a gradual relaxation of
the rules. The Home Office has been responsible for gambling policy and therefore social factors rather than revenue
implications have been the main consideration. The
National Lottery makes a significant reversal of that policy.
Furthermore, Mrs Virginia Bottomley, the then Heritage
Secretary, claimed when the Bill to introduce the National
Lottery was announced that it would not attract the gamblers: 'We expect it to attract new sections of the population, people who are willing to have a flutter knowing
that—win or lose—money will be going to good causes.'
The Council on Gambling immediately described this view
as naive and this has turned out to be correct.

For the Lottery to succeed it had to be promoted and the
Government has set about doing this most effectively. Control was switched to the Department of National Heritage
with a duty to maximise revenue rather than consider social
implications. And gaining money has proved to be the
major, if not the sole reason, for many people buying lottery
tickets. The reason people participate is in the hope of
winning. The percentage that goes to good causes is, I
believe, more of a sop to the conscience of the Government
and the organisers; it is also a good marketing tool. The
number of people who play using a form of elaborate 'lucky
numbers' is indicative of gambling.

It is quite clear too that Instants, with their 'heart-stop-
pers' and encouragement to buy more, clearly encourage
the potential gambler to try once more. The roll-over jackpot is yet another incentive to participate. Experience
already shows a strong correlation between jackpot size
and participation. Indeed the question of how much the

maximum prize can be is perhaps the most crucial factor in the whole thing. When the top prize is not won it is rolled over to the next week's draw. This can continue up to a maximum period of three weeks. Indications from Canada show potential problems here. In 1984 the jackpot was not won for several weeks, resulting in a very high potential sum available to the winner. During that particular week outlets reported double or triple the usual sales with reports of some people queuing for up to five hours to buy tickets. Many people apparently spent the equivalent of £50 a time. This surely flies in the face of those who believe that the Lottery will not attract gamblers and contradicts the comfortable notion that they will only invest what they can afford to lose.

'It could be you'

The frequency of advertising, television, radio and press comment also gives cause for concern. Much money is available and all publicity is generally good publicity. In reality the Lottery is an extremely bad bet yet people continue to participate in the hope of winning in the face of very long odds. Even the information about the odds of winning may not prove an adequate safeguard as participants consistently seem to underestimate the importance of those long odds and focus instead on the advertising telling them that 'it could be you'. This irrational behaviour may be self-justified in the (false) belief that their lucky numbers or system significantly reduces the odds. It may of course be the one and only desperate attempt to escape. While not wanting to deny that, I wonder what will happen over a period of time when many realise that these hopes actually promoted by the Government and Camelot prove to be false. Adverts present an image of success and happiness for the lucky winners thereby implying that people are fools if they do not participate. In fact, for the vast majority of people the best thing for them to do is to hold on to their money. Any suggestion that a spare, or even not-so-spare, pound should really buy a Lottery ticket is grossly misleading.

Problem gambling

In the run-up to the Lottery, even the Government implicitly implied that problems may well occur for some. 'For *most* people participation in the Lottery will provide a harmless form of entertainment. Many countries which have had a National Lottery for many years do not report any *major* adverse social effects.' However, evidence from the United States over the last thirty years does indicate first a new type of problem gambler, the lottery addict. Secondly, it also seems that the increased availability of this form of gambling has led to addictions to other forms. In one major survey researchers found that the amount of money spent on lotteries was a predictor of both loss of control (behavioural aspects such as hidden gambling, inability to resist the temptation, spending more than intended and a return to gambling after trying to give it up) and of problem gambling (losing time from work or school, borrowing money, illegal behaviour). Various characteristics such as impatience and impulsiveness were also seen to be predictors of such behaviour.

Studies confirm that gambling addiction leads to increased crime. A study by the University of Illinois concluded that were gambling to be brought to Chicago the criminal justice bill would soar by more than $1 billion. Dr Valerie Lorenz, Director of the National Center for Pathological Gambling in Baltimore, has no doubt about the contribution of large-scale lotteries to problem gambling: 'Ten years ago a female compulsive gambler was a rarity in treatment. Lottery addicts were virtually unheard of. Teenage compulsive gamblers were non-existent and compulsive gamblers amongst senior citizens were also a rarity a mere decade ago. Yet today all these compulsive gamblers abound in every state, at every Gamblers Anonymous meeting, at professional treatment programmes and in the criminal justice system.'[4] Dr Lorenz added that despite claims that lotteries are 'soft', addicts report the same feeling of excitement in placing bets and the same depression and despair after losing. This is invariably followed by a period of recovery when the desire to chase losses by improving their 'system' for picking numbers takes place. This can be followed by a decline in productivity, debt and even theft and suicide attempts. During the Center's first full year of operation (1988–89) seven per cent of compulsive gamblers stated that lotteries were their main form of gambling. By 1990 this figure had risen to twenty-two per cent and has continued to rise slowly since then.

Iain Brown, lecturer in psychology at the University of Glasgow and a specialist in compulsive gambling, said 'We've seen what happens in other parts of the world. It can have the effect of unhinging people's grip on reality. It creates a false dream state and paralyses action because people expect manna from heaven. The people who are most susceptible are those leading drab and depressing lives. It becomes a substitute for hope. I'd call it a tax on poverty and despair.'[5] See how this is already echoed in the quote of the newsagent who sold tickets to the man who killed himself because he thought he had missed the jackpot: 'People become obsessed by the National Lottery. For some of my customers it is all they seem to live for. They spend their last pennies on it each week.'

Salvation by Lottery

In an intelligent and thought-provoking leader article in *The Independent*, it was said:

Once we sought salvation in religion. Now ten million prayers are raised for a National Lottery jackpot. In an inner-city corner shop impoverished pensioners and despairing dads queue to put money they cannot afford into a competition that statistically they cannot win. Like Jack in the story they hand their livelihood over for a handful of beans—except there will be no beanstalk. Constant fantasising about how vast sums of unearned dosh would transform their lives corrodes the ability to live in the present. And many are becoming gamblers for the first time. Unlike betting on the horse or hound or filling in the pools, expertise confers no advantage in the Lottery—all clearly stand an equal chance. As a result many who never enter a betting shop or return a slip to Littlewoods are being drawn into gambling—and gambling addiction.

Democracy allows people to make their own decisions about the balance of advantage. In an incredibly short period of time the Lottery has become a national institution that cannot be uninvented. Nevertheless here is a prediction. In fifteen years or so the Chief Medical Officer will issue a report detailing the damage done by excessive gambling on the Lottery. This report will make one or all of the following recommendations—that all tickets carry a health warning, that all advertising makes it clear just how preposterous the odds are, and that the National Lottery itself should fund a national health education campaign by Gamblers Anonymous. Perhaps we shouldn't wait.'[6]

Maximising Lottery profits

Another problem is that of a lottery maturing. As it does so the increase in revenue slows down. This creates considerable pressure for profit—and operators seek to increase participation rates. Whereas in the case of our Lottery the participation rates are already high, others can tend to lead to advertising strategies aimed at converting casual users into regular ones. New games and new technologies such as telephone betting and video lotteries for use in arcades can also be used to maintain revenue growth. Such pressures can only increase the potential for addictive gambling. It is my belief that current safeguards go nowhere near far enough to prevent this happening in the future.

Personal tragedies

A fifty-year-old reformed gambler knew better than most that he needed help when he spent £120 on the National Lottery in one week. The temptation had proved too great and so he turned to Gamblers Anonymous. 'Buying the Lottery Instants was like standing at the edge of a whirlpool,' he said. 'I started with bets of no more than £1 at a time but it began to accelerate and I felt I was being sucked in.' His decline began with the first big jackpot of £17 million. 'When there was a roll-over I started to spend more than I could afford. When the Instants came out it was so easy to walk into a shop and buy them with my newspaper.' Soon he found himself feeling that same old unwanted thrill.

A similar story came from a clerical worker in Edinburgh who had been a compulsive gambler twenty years ago but restarted with the Lottery. Research by the Henley Centre that has studied lotteries in Britain, Canada and Ireland found a core of such committed players in each country. They tend to come from lower income backgrounds. Typical is a jobless young lady from Glasgow who borrows up to £60 to buy Instants every week. 'I don't want to buy them but I can't help it,' she said, 'but the tickets are a possible route out of here.'

For many too the urge to spend on the Lottery retains its allure long after the dream of winning has turned sour. A thirty-year-old man has spent his entire winnings of £48,000 in four months on a car, holiday and improvements to his flat. He is now forced to try and find a new job after giving up his position as a security guard in the euphoria of his win. He continues to spend £15 on tickets every week.

The Samaritans, too, have begun to receive calls at the peak times of Saturday night and Sunday morning from people whose depression has been deepened by picking the wrong numbers. Even the Gaming Board has called for research into possible links between compulsive gambling and the National Lottery. Lady Littler, their chairwoman, said that there were tremendous temptations to go on and on buying scratch cards. 'If you have a small win you are tempted to blow it on more cards and if you do not you are tempted to go on and have another go.'

Debt

An investigation by *The Sunday Express* found that the dream of easy money is so powerful that buying Lottery tickets has in some cases taken over from day-to-day expenditure on essentials. It found there was evidence of mounting rent arrears and mortgage debt because people are spending more than they can afford on the Lottery and Instants. Housing officers in Taunton reported this as a key factor in rent arrears that were ten per cent higher than a year ago. A council spokesman said that people with the least means are the ones to whom the dream of a Lottery win is most important. 'Paying the rent is boring and winning the Lottery means the end to all financial troubles. So it's no contest. But it can only be played at the expense of other things.' Top city mortgage analyst, Rob Thomas, also said that the Lottery was to blame for an increase in short-term mortgage arrears.

Values

Every Bill introduced into Parliament, and especially if it becomes law, says something about the values of our society.

What sort of message then is our Government sending out by promoting the Lottery?

Economists Clotfelter and Cook are quite clear:

> There is more to selling lottery tickets than persuading the public that playing is a good investment. At a more basic level the sales job may be viewed as an education in values, teaching that gambling is a benign or even virtuous activity that offers an escape from the dreariness of work and limited means. Not only does lottery advertising endorse gambling per se but it also endorses the dream of easy wealth that motivates gambling. The ads are unabashedly materialistic and their message is a slightly subversive one—that success is just a matter of picking the right numbers. The gospel of wealth based on sweat and a little bit of luck is replaced by one based on luck alone. Needless to say waiting for fortune to smile is not the formula for success that is usually taught.[7]

My first reaction on reading this was: what on earth does this message convey to our children? But it affects adults too and it affects them now. Recently we had a call on the Credit Action helpline from a man addicted to the Lottery. He was a low-paid manual worker. He didn't like his job and he didn't like where he lived and he had negative equity on his property. 'My life is so mundane' he complained. 'I am nine weeks in arrears with my mortgage so I might as well be ten weeks behind and use the money for Lottery tickets again. At least if I win I will be out of here and never have to pay the—mortgage again.'

I can see that for some, sources of hope are hard to find. But policies offering real hope need to be found rather than a Lottery which offers initial false dreams and eventual further disillusionment to the millions who are struggling in our country. The Lottery will not make the country any richer. It is currently a more popular way than taxation of redistributing wealth. A nation that relies on hard work is usually prosperous. A government that switches priorities to luck should be really concerned that it is undermining a valuable plank of the nation's very being.

Greed

Another question that needs answering is that when something depends on greed to be successful, can it be regarded as morally acceptable? I think you can dismiss the 'good causes' argument because if you want to give you can do so easily and select your own preferences as well. It is also clear that when there is a roll-over jackpot ticket sales increase significantly thus increasing the likelihood of gambling addiction. I do not see how this can be morally justifiable because it must mean that the pressures are such, particularly for the desperate, that they will certainly overcommit themselves. It is clearly a sad sign also when the 132 millionaires that the Lottery had created so far said that their biggest regrets were that they didn't win sooner and that they didn't win more.

Public opinion

A very large percentage of the population approved of the National Lottery when it started and there are still many who cling to that view. But with all the criticism that has been levelled at it there are signs of opinion turning and this was in fact pointed out in a *Daily Mail* leader in December 1995. The late Marjorie Proops who was on the 1978 Royal Commission that looked into the National Lottery is one who changed her mind. She asked, 'Will you forgive us? We were naive and very foolish. If I had my time again my answer would be no.'

Camelot themselves have shown nervousness in the past that public opinion might turn against the Lottery. They lobbied delegates ahead of a critical debate at the Liberal Democrats Conference and they also launched an advertising onslaught at the time of its first anniversary in which it emphasised the benefits that it brings to 'good causes'. They employ a team of ten to deal with factual enquiries about the Lottery as well as an external P.R. company and a public affairs team that handles the more awkward questions. They have admitted that the 'It could be you' advert was specially chosen because it veiled the I in 14 million chance of winning the Lottery in simple optimism. Mr Rigg (Camelot's Director of Communications) said, 'What the public responded to was the idea that they could win and the odds were not against them. Every time we considered the campaign we tested it against the words 'simple, easy and fun'.'

Areas of concern

Sadly, many do not seem to realise the dangers that being addicted to the National Lottery can bring. Credit Action is particularly concerned that there seems to be so little Christian guidance in this area. There are four areas of concern.

Fall-off in charitable giving

Only a very small amount of the money spent on Lottery tickets (5.6p) goes to charity. However, it is quite clear that many people, including some Christians, justify their position by stating that some of the proceeds go to charity. Many Christian organisations rely heavily on the general public for support and Credit Action is aware of several Christian charities that are under intense financial pressure and many feel things can only get worse as a result of the Lottery. The number of people giving regularly to charity has fallen from eighty-one per cent to sixty-seven per cent since the introduction of the Lottery.

Poor witness

What makes a bad situation worse is that we are aware of some Christian churches and charities that are applying for grants to the Lotteries Board. Given the pressures that some of these organisations are under the temptation is understandable. However, we believe that the ends cannot always be used to justify the means and we particularly applaud groups such as the Methodist Church and the Oasis Trust who have specifically stated the reasons why they will not be applying.

Causing others to stumble

Many people can probably afford to lose the odd pound or two on a Lottery ticket without it causing them too much damage. But this does not mean it is all right to do so. The Bible says, 'Whoever loves his brother lives in the light, and there is nothing in him to make him stumble.'[8] There are many people today struggling to make ends meet. Wasting money on gambling is bad stewardship. We are in effect saying we would rather throw money away than use it to meet the needs of our neighbour. The Bible says, 'People who want to get rich fall into temptation and a trap and into many foolish and harmful desires that plunge men into ruin and destruction. For the love of money is a root of all kinds of evil.'[9]

Storing up treasure

The key question is where do we want to store up treasures? The Bible makes it very clear that we have to choose; there is no place for compromise. 'Do not store up for yourselves treasures on earth, where moth and rust destroy, and where thieves break in and steal. But store up for yourselves treasures in heaven where moth and rust do not destroy, and where thieves do not break in and steal. For where your treasure is, there your heart will be also . . . No-one can serve two masters . . . You cannot serve both God and Money.'[10]

Money and the desire for riches are likely to be the major drawbacks in our relationship with Christ. The dangers of this are clear. Mark's Gospel tells us that it is easier for a camel to go through the eye of a needle than for a rich man to enter the kingdom of God[11]—and in wordly terms almost all of us in the West are rich!

All of us need to be aware of just how harmful gambling can be. We should heed Ezekiel's warning, 'Their silver and gold will not be able to save them in the day of the Lord's wrath. They will not satisfy their hunger or fill their stomachs with it, for it has made them stumble into sin.'[12]

I could not conclude this chapter in any better way than by leaving the reader to ponder the following quote from John White: 'It is want of faith that makes us opt for earthly rather than heavenly treasure. If we really believed in celestial treasures who amongst us would be so stupid as to buy gold. We just do not believe. If people believed in Heaven they would spend all their time preparing for permanent residence there but nobody does.'[13]

I believe that Jesus taught us to love people and to use money to help those less fortunate than ourselves. Sadly, gambling is all about 'self' and is thus far removed from Christ's teaching.

Notes

1. Blake W. *Augaries of innocence*. New York: E D Hirsch, 1964.
2. Orwell G. *Nineteen eighty-four*. Oxford: Clarendon Press, 1984.
3. Fitzherbert L. *Rowntree Report on the National Lottery*. London: Directory of Social Change, 1995.
4. Lorenz V. London: *Daily Mail*, October 1995.
5. Brown I. London: *The Times*, May 1995.
6. London: *The Independent*, April 1995.
7. Clotfelter CT, Cook PJ. *Selling hope: State Lotteries in America*. Cambridge, Mass; Harvard University Press, 1989.

8. 1 John 2:10.
9. 1 Timothy 6:8–10.
10. Matthew 6:19–21, 24–25.
11. Mark 10:24.
12. Ezekiel 7:10.
13. White J. *Money isn't God – So why are we worshipping it?* Leicester: IVP, 1993.

CHAPTER NINE

NATIONAL PRIORITIES FOR HEALTH

Ian McColl

Lord McColl is Professor of Surgery at the United Medical and Dental Schools of Guy's and St Thomas's Hospitals. He was Parliamentary Private Secretary to the Prime Minister from 1994–97.

At the turn of the century Dr Alfred Salter emerged from Guy's Hospital having won most of the prizes and had the prospect of a brilliant career in hospital medicine. He chose instead to work as a general practitioner in Bermondsey. His Christian commitment to improving the health of the people of the borough was so intense that he and his wife decided to live in Bermondsey, one of the first doctors so to do. This decision was not unrelated to the subsequent death of his daughter at the age of twelve. At that time probably half his patients were either unfed or ill-fed and the amount of illness was appalling. He set to work to improve the health of the whole district. However hard he worked, it became clear to him that the excellence of his medicine was having no effect on the overall health of the people. He and his wife entered local politics and were responsible for the planting of trees all over Bermondsey and such was the success of this endeavour that in the 1930s Bermondsey was visited by many dignitaries from overseas

141

to see what was described as 'the garden city of the world'. In spite of all these efforts, he failed to improve the health of the people. As a last resort he entered Parliament in 1922 and became the first Labour MP for Bermondsey. He was greatly respected for his high principles. He could hardly have failed to have seen the deleterious effects of alcohol abuse, not only among his patients but upon the Members of Parliament, and often harangued them on this important part of preventative medicine.

He was horrified at the outbreak of World War 2 and yet it was the introduction of food rationing in 1939 which improved the health of the whole district. Dr Salter died in 1945 having served as an MP until that time. The destruction of Bermondsey by Nazi bombing dramatically dealt with the slums and the subsequent rebuilding of the district. This together with the cure of underfeeding or incorrect feeding did wonders for the health of that riparian borough. It often comes as a surprise for some medical students that the health of a nation is more dependent on public health and social issues than the clinical activities of doctors. The reduction in tuberculosis over this century in this country has much more to do with nutrition and housing than medicines.

National priorities

It is a simple matter to determine national priorities for health and to ensure that the majority of people are fully aware of these priorities and how to achieve them. The problem is that although most people know how to enjoy good health, large numbers of them ignore the advice and live a lifestyle which leads to poor health and often to an early death. This state of affairs is as old as the hills. The Old Testament is full of excellent advice on how to be healthy but countless generations have ignored those simple rules for healthy living.

One of the earliest clinical trials was initiated by Daniel and his companions soon after they were selected for training for the court of King Nebuchadnezzar. They did not regard the King's food and wine as conducive to good health and started a ten-day trial of a high roughage diet in the form of vegetables with water. After ten days it was obvious that Daniel's regime was superior.

Individual responsibilities for health

In many Western countries with developed health services, many people fail to recognise the need for personal responsibility in health care. There is a great comfort in having a free health service at the point of demand which will pick up the bill if we need it. While some illnesses obviously cannot be avoided, even with the largest killers, cancer and heart disease, there is much that individuals can do to avoid the risk.

Although there are differences of opinion on the recipe for good health, there is agreement that there should be absolutely no smoking at all, that a seventy kilogram (eleven stone) man should limit his alcohol intake to three units a day and a lady of the same weight to two units a day. Body weight should be kept to within normal range and this can be facilitated by having a low-fat and high-roughage diet which satisfies hunger and reduces the instance of a large number of diseases. Patients who are overweight often claim that they 'eat nothing'—nothing could be further from the truth. We are what we eat.

Regular exercise, preferably enjoyable, should be the order of the day. Personal dental care and an adequate fluoride intake in drinking water, tablets or toothpaste will substantially decrease caries and dental expenses. Countless lives are completely wrecked by cannabis, amphetamine, heroin and other dangerous drugs but it is important to point out that all addictive drugs must be avoided.

Creeping addiction can result from supposedly innocuous drugs like dihydrocodeine and codeine.

Daily prayer and reading of Scriptures promote a healthy mind and spirit. In a busy life this may present problems but there are various ways of achieving this. While listening in the car to a tape recording of selected New Testament readings, it is difficult to shout abuse to passing motorists! It is usually best to avoid opening mail too late at night which may interfere with sleep. Never let the sun sink on your anger.

Compliance with these principles and those enunciated in the Good Book make for a long and contented life. It is encouraging that these rules are often endorsed by international organisations, such as the World Health Organisation, which recommended faithfulness for life to one partner. The rules are quite straightforward: the problem is how to encourage people to abide by them.

Importance of education

The home should be one of the main places where correct conduct should be instilled into the children in terms of a balanced diet, personal dental care, adequate exercise, avoiding all smoking and a clear guidance on the danger of drugs and alcohol abuse. Much long-term illness, both psychiatric and physical, is induced into thousands of children by physical and sexual abuse which often pollutes the whole of their lives.

The values inculcated at home should be reinforced at school. Recent Governments have acknowledged the importance of instilling values in the young through the educational system. At a conference in Oxford in January 1994, the then Secretary of State the Rt Hon John Patten MP stated: 'Values lie at the heart of education and schools should teach them.' Recent education legislation has enabled the Government to halt the progressive tide in favour of a more traditional and family-based approach to values. It was commonly thought at the turn of the century that the answer to society's problems was increasing education but the evils of the two World Wars shattered that illusion. What of course is needed in addition to education is a radical change in people's attitudes.

Role of the media

The media could help to promote the health of the nation and from time to time they do so. For instance, the radio programme *The Archers* devoted one episode to the importance of a high-roughage diet. The message was blended cleverly into the programme, which was therefore acceptable to the listeners, whereas a straightforward propaganda programme telling people what they should eat would be rejected. The media, of course, could be of enormous help but all too frequently they only highlight or invent what they regard as sensational news.

Voluntary organisations

Voluntary organisations do much valuable work in improving the health of many. Their work in health and personal social services work is acknowledged by the Government who have supported them through the provision of Section 64 grants. Take as an example the AIDS charity ACET which has distributed over half a million copies of its booklet *HIV Facts for Life* to schools throughout the UK. Supported by the Association of British Insurers, many lives have been positively impacted by this provision of responsible sex education literature. Even in some of the hardest areas of health promotion and care, namely with drug users and addicts, voluntary service provision is making an impressive contribution to the health of the population. I had the privilege of paying a visit to Yeldall Manor, a drug rehabilitation centre, to witness first-hand the outstanding work being undertaken for those suffering from addictive disorders.

Role of Government

What can Government do to help? They have defined the national priorities for health in a consultative document published in 1991 called *The Health of the Nation* which seeks to define the problems, suggests targets and proposes solutions. For example, it points out that much heart disease could be prevented by healthier life-styles and suggests that we should aim to reduce by thirty per cent the deaths of those under sixty-five years from coronary heart disease by the year 2000. They suggest that with the help of screening, the mortality from breast disease should be reduced by 25 per cent by the year 2000. It also suggests ways of improving the environment by reducing the pollution of the air by vehicles and complying with EC directives to end significant discharges of untreated sewage.

Government has encouraged the use of lead-free petrol by making it cheaper, taxes have been increased on smoking and alcohol which will discourage their consumption, but these are measures which tend to be unpopular with those who smoke and drink. By the same token it could be argued that Government should seek to make good food cheaper, thereby making unhealthy products relatively dearer. There should be some way of discouraging those large foodstores which reduce their prices of junk foods such as crisps, sugary soft drinks, ice cream and cakes, in order to attract the customers where they would often buy more of the inappropriate type of food.

Road pollution and congestion could be eased if encouragement were given to use bicycles rather than cars but steps would have to be taken to make it easier and safer for cyclists.

The European Community should be encouraged to promote healthy eating by encouraging the reduction of the cost of healthy foods. This could be helped by withdrawing the £1 billion subsidy per year which is given to enable the growth of European tobacco which is of such poor quality that half of it has to be destroyed and the other half sold to the developing nations, the latter being a danger which should be avoided.

In the past, legislation has been successful in eliminating the old 'pea soup' fog by prohibiting the burning of coal in cities. In one night in the winter of 1953 over 3,000 people died in London alone during one of these fogs.

Compulsory wearing of seat belts has substantially reduced death and injury in road traffic accidents. This campaign has been so successful that the number of kidney donors has been thereby reduced. This has been a further stimulus to the Government to encourage more people to carry donor cards to facilitate a harvest of suitable organs for transplantation. The Government campaign to discourage drinking and driving has also helped.

It has to be said that there has been an extraordinary degree of opposition to some of these measures. The proposed fluoridation of drinking water raised enormous opposition in some quarters on the basis of an infringement of liberty. In retrospect, it might have been better to have labelled the campaign a 'redistribution of the level of fluoride in drinking water' as some districts had more than others and the object was to provide fair shares for all!

Vaccination programme

A minister of health in the eighties was asked by the medical profession to devise an incentive scheme to promote vaccination. The arrangement was an incentive of £2,145 if ninety per cent of the childhood vaccinations were carried out in an average size practice, whereas only £715 was paid if only seventy per cent were vaccinated. For pre-school boosters the corresponding figures for the higher rate were £630 and for the lower rate £210. Similarly, for cervical cytology the maximum payable to a general practitioner in a practice with an average of 430 eligible patients aged twenty-five to sixty-four was £2,415 per partner if an eighty per cent goal was achieved, whereas the figure for fifty per cent was £805. This scheme produced considerable opposition at first but it was soon found to be effective.

An emergency situation arose at the end of 1994 when it became clear that a measles epidemic was imminent and an enormous vaccination programme was rapidly undertaken. It turned out to be a great success and in January 1995, when the epidemic was due to strike, only six cases of measles were reported. This triumph of organisation and altruism was scarcely reported by the media.

On the international scene, the determined effort to eliminate smallpox has at last succeeded and demonstrates that when enough effort and organisation is put into such a project, success is likely. The elimination of some fatal and distressing congenital conditions is now possible. This new field of endeavour raises all kinds of ethical problems which have to be carefully examined as they arise.

Conclusions

Although there have been many set-backs, disappointments and lack of support from the media at large, generally the health of the nation continues to improve. Perhaps more exciting is a growing realisation that while the medical, nursing and allied professions can do much to alleviate the suffering of many, further advances in preventative medicine are, in the final analysis, the responsibility of every individual.

It is rapidly dawning on many that a health service cannot solve all our health problems. Despite this, some politicians continue to use the health service as a political football to win votes, and the importance of health becomes a secondary issue. As the change in thinking occurs, there are many years of ignorance to strip away; however, this revolution in thinking is gathering pace. Fifteen years ago, a similar revolution began with regards to the Earth and the environment in which we live. Now, and not a moment too soon, we have also begun to look at ourselves and ask how we as individuals can look forward to a healthy sustained future.

CHAPTER TEN

EUTHANASIA

Robert Twycross

Dr Twycross is Macmillan Clinical Reader in Palliative Medicine and Honorary Consultant Physician at Sir Michael Sobell House, Churchill Hospital, Oxford, a WHO Collaborating Centre for Palliative Cancer Care. He is an acknowledged authority on palliative care and has also written widely on euthanasia.

Since the days of Hippocrates, doctors have undertaken never to destroy life deliberately, but will endeavour to sustain life when, from a biological point of view, it is sustainable. A doctor, however, has a dual responsibility— to sustain life and to relieve suffering. Medicine must be practised with the recognition that ultimately all patients will die. To claim that a doctor must sustain life 'at all costs' is biologically untenable. The overriding medical responsibility at the end of a person's life is to relieve suffering. A doctor has no legal or ethical obligation to use drugs, techniques or apparatus if their use can best be described as prolonging the process or distress of dying. It is against this background that the topic of euthanasia must be discussed.

Definition

Euthanasia literally means 'good death', that is death without suffering. For many years, however, the word has been used as a synonym for 'mercy killing': 'The compassion-motivated, deliberate, rapid and painless termination of the life of someone afflicted with an incurable and progressive disease. If performed at the dying person's request or with that person's consent, euthanasia is voluntary; otherwise it is non-voluntary.'[1]

Discussion has been complicated by the use of the term 'passive euthanasia' to describe 'letting nature take its course' by not applying futile medical treatment.[1] Because it is not deliberate death acceleration, however, it should not be described as euthanasia. Further, the use of the term derives from a failure to distinguish between the aims of acute medicine and terminal care. As already indicated, priorities change when a patient is expected to die within a few weeks or months; the primary aim is no longer to sustain life but to make the life which remains as comfortable and as meaningful as possible.

It has been said that the ethical justification for 'letting nature take its course' relies on the doctrine of 'acts and omissions'. This states that, in certain situations, failure to perform an act (e.g. prescribe an antibiotic for a patient with terminal cancer who develops pneumonia) is less bad than performing a different act (e.g. administering a lethal overdose) which has identical predictable consequences. In other words, it is more reprehensible to kill someone than to allow a person to die. This doctrine is irrelevant, however, in the present context and, as stated, is based on a naive understanding of clinical realities. Since death is inevitable for all of us, a doctor is bound ultimately to 'let nature take its course'.

Acute and terminal illness are distinct pathophysiological conditions. In the former, provided the patient survives the initial crisis, recovery is brought about largely by natural forces of healing; in the latter, these forces become progressively less effective as physical dissolution proceeds. In practice, therefore, the argument revolves round the question of *effective interference* and not the doctrine of 'acts and omissions'. Thus, what is appropriate in one situation may be inappropriate in the other. Antibiotics, nasogastric tubes, blood transfusions and cardiopulmonary resuscitation are all primarily supportive measures for use in acute illness to assist a patient through a critical period towards recovery of health. To use such measures in the terminally ill, with no expectancy of a return to health, is generally inappropriate and is therefore, by definition, not only bad medicine but also unethical.

If the distinction between acute and terminal illness is ignored, however, the situation will not be assessed in terms of what is biologically appropriate (and therefore in the patient's best interest) but will be seen as a question of 'to treat or not to treat?' A failure to resolve what appears to be an ethical dilemma commonly results in additional, unnecessary suffering for the patient as inappropriate life-sustaining measures are continued.

Contrary to popular belief, it is generally possible to relieve pain in terminal cancer either completely or to a great extent.[2,3,4,5] Further, it is seldom necessary to dull consciousness in order to achieve adequate relief. The success of modern methods of pain management, exemplified in the hospice (palliative care) movement in the UK and elsewhere, is attested to by the Voluntary Euthanasia Society itself:

> The circumstances in which people die vary widely. A small number have the good fortune to be cared for in [hospices], organized and administered with the specific aim of making their patients 'fairly comfortable' in their last days rather than attempting to cure them when that seems out of the question

. . . Experience has shown that in the sympathetic and some-times surprisingly cheerful atmosphere it is possible for a large proportion of patients (many of them with cancer) to be 'gentled' along in comparative comfort, so that they are able to face death, when it comes, with a quiet mind—unafraid . . . Even if euthanasia were permissible to these patients probably very few would wish to avail themselves of it.[6]

The term 'indirect euthanasia' has been used to describe the administration of analgesics to patients with terminal cancer. This is incorrect; giving a drug to lessen pain cannot be equated with giving a lethal dose deliberately to end life. There is general agreement that should life be shortened by the use of such drugs, it is an acceptable risk in the circum-stances. This is called the principle of double effect. In other words, if measures taken to relieve pain (or other distress) cause the death of a patient, it is morally acceptable provided the doctor's intention was to relieve the distress and not to kill the patient. English case law is equally clear:

A doctor who is aiding the sick and the dying does not have to calculate in minutes or even in hours, and perhaps not in days or weeks, the effect upon a patient's life of the medicines which he administers or else be in peril of a charge of murder. If the first purpose of medicine, the restoration of health, can no longer be achieved, there is still much for a doctor to do, and he is entitled to do all that is proper and necessary to relieve pain and suffering, even if the measures he takes may inci-dentally shorten life.[7]

It is important to remember that all treatment has an inherent risk. Although a greater risk is acceptable in more extreme circumstances, it is axiomatic that effective measures which carry less risk to life must normally be used. Thus, in an extreme situation, it may be acceptable to render a patient unconscious but it is still unacceptable to cause death deliberately. It should be emphasised, however, that morphine and related drugs (correctly used) are much safer than often supposed. There is much circumstantial evidence which suggests that those whose pain is relieved outlive those whose rest and nutrition continue to be disturbed by severe pain.

A Christian perspective

The debate about euthanasia within a 'plural' society must be conducted mainly along pragmatic, utilitarian and consequentialist lines. To argue from mutually exclusive philosophical positions will never lead to the consensus which every society must seek to achieve.

'We treat animals better than we do humans' and 'if he were an animal, he'd be put down' are comments which recur too often for comfort. Although on one level they can be easily countered, such statements reflect a depth of compassion and anguish which can easily be lost or ignored in a detached discussion of Christian principles.

The fundamental argument in favour of euthanasia is 'the patient's right to self-determination'. The fundamental counter-argument is that patient autonomy does not extend to a right to medically-assisted suicide/euthanasia. These two viewpoints ('man as master' v 'man as steward') are not reconcilable. Although autonomy is important in Christian thinking, the overall witness of the Bible and Christian tradition is that *human life is made in the image of God and is not ours to dispose of as we think fit.* In other words, we hold our lives in stewardship from God. There is, therefore, a limit to personal autonomy. As a doctor, the patient's life is entrusted to me in stewardship and I am answerable to God for the manner in which I exercise that trust. This view is not just based on a few 'proof texts' but stems from the doctrine of creation, incarnation and redemption, and the belief that the Christian believer is, in a special way, 'the temple of the Holy Spirit'. Thus, some of the questions surrounding persistent vegetative state, suicide and euthanasia are beset by tensions which are to a great extent unique to the Christian faith[8] and to other belief systems which hold comparable views (e.g. Judaism and Islam).

Discussion concerning euthanasia generally assumes that death means oblivion. For the Christian and for many others, this is not so. On the other hand, to make 'eternal destiny' the crucial argument in the case against euthanasia is generally counter-productive. Even so, the Christian will wonder whether God may have things to say to a dying person which could be precluded if death was deliberately accelerated.[8] For the Christian, the mode of dying is eternally important; it is not merely the snuffing out of a spluttering candle.

Those in favour of euthanasia often stress that there is a level of existence where most, if not all, people would wish not to be kept alive. If conscious, they might actively ask for assistance to die, emphasising that life no longer has meaning or purpose for them. Patients in irreversible coma (more than six months?) would be one category and persistent vegetative state another. Possibly, also advanced motor neurone disease (creeping paralysis) or when cancer erodes the face and replaces familiar features with a malodorous, ulcerating, fungating mass, or when a similar process affects the perineum and results in distressing, humiliating double incontinence. These are powerful images and must be acknowledged by those who say 'no' to euthanasia. Palliative care *cannot* 'sanitise' all forms of dying. Indeed, even though opposed to euthanasia, I would say that

- a doctor who has never been tempted to kill a patient probably has had limited clinical experience or is not able to empathise with those who suffer;
- a doctor who leaves a patient to suffer intolerably is morally more reprehensible than the doctor who opts for euthanasia.

Requests for euthanasia

Requests for euthanasia are uncommon.[9] Further, in the experience of hospice staff: 'Most of those who demand help to die are asking for help to live.' It is critically important to hear the cry for life underlying a patient's 'lament'.[10] It is necessary, therefore, to identify the reason(s) for the demand and to respond accordingly. Reasons vary but include:

- unrelieved severe pain or other physical distress;
- fear of future intolerable pain or other physical distress;
- fear of being kept alive with machines and tubes at a time when quality of life would be unacceptably low;
- a short-term adjustment disorder, i.e. temporary despair on discovering one has a fatal disease with limited life expectancy;
- feeling a burden on one's family, friends or society generally;
- feeling unwanted by family, friends or people generally;
- depression (meaning a depressive illness, not just sadness);
- a fixed sense of hopelessness which cannot be explained in terms of any of the above, and which usually stems from an atheistic view of life with no concept of personal survival beyond the grave.

Except perhaps in this final scenario, it is generally possible to take sufficient corrective measures to lead to a change of mind by the patient.

Case history

A sixty-eight-year-old retired railway porter became increasingly unwell as a result of lung cancer. He began to abuse his relatives, withdrew from social contacts and repeatedly threatened suicide. When admitted, he was dirty, unkempt and for the previous six weeks had been virtually bedfast and alone because of weakness. He had no appetite, was constipated and had widespread pain. He said he would like to put his head into a gas oven. He was prescribed cortisone and an antidepressant. A week later, he was asked if he still wanted to gas himself. He replied, 'I don't want to go home.' It then came out that he was living in a flat at the top of his son's house and that the relationship between them was more than strained. On no account did he wish to go back there and was relieved when told that he need not. Within two weeks he was symptom-free and fully mobile; he definitely no longer wished to die. A month after admission he suddenly became confused, had to be helped back to bed and died an hour later.

The slippery slope

The 'slippery slope' is a term commonly used to refer to the danger of voluntary euthanasia for terminally ill patients leading to nonvoluntary euthanasia and/or extending to patients who are not terminally ill. Experience in the Netherlands illustrates the slippery slope effect in practice. The Dutch Royal Decree concerning euthanasia came into effect in early 1994. Although euthanasia remains a criminal offence in the Netherlands, the Decree states how doctors may avoid prosecution in four sets of circumstances:

- request to terminate life by patients suffering from a physical disorder;
- request to terminate life by patients suffering from a psychiatric disorder;
- active termination of life without express request in patients suffering from a physical disorder;
- active termination of life without express request in patients suffering from a psychiatric disorder.

The fact that the Decree covers both voluntary and non-voluntary euthanasia and both physical and psychiatric disorders is unequivocal confirmation that the Dutch have already slipped down the slope. It does not make sense, therefore, for those in the Netherlands in favour of euthanasia to argue strongly against such a likelihood.[11,12] Indeed, the Report of a Commission set up by the Dutch Government (the Remmelink Report) confirmed several years ago that nonvoluntary euthanasia already occurs in the Netherlands.[13,14] In the majority of cases, there is no explicit request by the patient.[15]

It is disturbing, therefore, that nearly half of a group of doctors recently surveyed in the UK would welcome the liberties extended to the medical profession in the Netherlands in relation to voluntary euthanasia.[16] Reference to the House of Lord's Select Committee on Medical Ethics[17] is apposite:

> We do not think it is possible to set secure limits on voluntary euthanasia . . . We took account of the present situation in the Netherlands; indeed some of us visited that country and talked to doctors, lawyers and others. We returned feeling uncomfortable, especially in the light of evidence indicating that nonvoluntary euthanasia . . . was commonly performed, admittedly in incompetent terminally ill patients. We also learned of one case in which voluntary euthanasia was accepted by both doctors and lawyers in a physically fit 50 year-old woman alleged to be suffering from intolerable mental stress.[18]

The woman referred to above was divorced, had had one son die by suicide and the other of cancer. Euthanasia for morbid grief/depression? This is where the Dutch experience has taken them.

In my opinion, it is naive to say, 'It could never happen here.' It can and it will unless there is a strong continuing stand by officialdom against euthanasia in any form. Remember, too, it was the medical profession which introduced nonvoluntary euthanasia into Germany in the

1920s.[19,20] All the Nazis did was to extend the concept on political grounds.

Conclusions

I have been a hospice doctor for over twenty-five years. During this time, my opinions on many issues both within and outside clinical practice have changed. One that has not changed, however, is my belief that it would be a disaster for the medical profession to cross the Rubicon and use pharmacological means to precipitate death intentionally. When everything is taken into account (physical, psychological, social and spiritual), euthanasia is *not* the answer, either for the patient, the family, the professional carers or society. Indeed, to espouse euthanasia in the light of all that I have learned and experienced during this time would be to betray the thousands of patients that I have looked after.

If the reasons for my conviction were to be examined, those in favour of euthanasia might well be able to say of each individual reason, 'That's no reason for opposing voluntary euthanasia.' In so doing, the logic of my position might seem to be destroyed. But only *seemingly* because, even if no one objection were deemed sufficient, I believe that they add up to an overwhelming case against (Table 1). This is why I applaud the conclusion of the House of Lord's Select Committee on Medical Ethics (1994) that there should be no change in the law to permit euthanasia:

[There is] not sufficient reason to weaken society's prohibition of intentional killing which is the cornerstone of law and of social relationships. Individual cases cannot reasonably establish the foundation of a policy which would have such serious and widespread repercussions. The issue of euthanasia is one in which the interests of the individual cannot be separated from those of society as a whole.[18]

Table 1 Pragmatic reasons for opposing euthanasia

Reason	Comment
Many requests stem from inadequate symptom relief.	Patients no longer ask when symptoms are relieved adequately.
Other requests relate to a sense of uselessness or feeling a burden.	Good palliative care restores hope by giving the patient a sense of direction.
Persistent requests often reflect a depressive illness.	Depression requires specific treatment, not euthanasia.
Patients frequently change their minds.	Many patients have transient periods of despair.
Prognosis is often uncertain.	Some patients live for years longer than originally anticipated.
A 'euthanasia mentality' results in voluntary euthanasia extending to nonvoluntary euthanasia.	This is indisputably the case in the Netherlands.[21]
Once permitted, euthanasia will not be restricted to the terminally ill.	Euthanasia commentators urge a wider remit[22] and euthanasia for mental suffering in the nonphysically ill is now accepted in the Netherlands.[23]
If voluntary euthanasia was permitted, elderly and terminally ill patients would feel 'at risk'.	Anecdotal evidence and the results of a survey of elderly people in the Netherlands lend support to this contention.[24]

Reason	Comment
Pressure on doctors from relatives to impose euthanasia on patients could be irresistible.	The Remmelink Report demonstrates that relatives do put pressure on doctors.[14]
Doctors who find it hard to cope with 'failure' will tend to impose euthanasia.	Anecdotal evidence from the Netherlands supports this contention.[25]
Voluntary euthanasia will remove the incentive to improve standards of palliative care.	Palliative care is still in its infancy in the Netherlands; improvements are undoubtedly being hindered by the acceptance of voluntary euthanasia.[26]
Budgetary constraints are seen by some to be a compelling reason for legalising euthanasia.	This view has been expressed by both doctors[27] and economists.

Instead, the Committee urged the development and growth of palliative care services throughout the UK. The same conclusion was reached by the British Medical Association.[28,29]

Likewise, I share the sentiments of the Nursing Forum on AIDS of the Royal College of Nursing:

[We are] vehemently opposed to any initiatives which would seek to legalise euthanasia for people with AIDS. Such legalised death would encourage the prevalent ignorance about the condition and decelerate the research being undertaken into this condition. It could also have serious ramifications for other chronically and terminally ill people. Rather, medicine and nursing should grasp the opportunity to pursue education about this condition, and gain information and knowledge so that symptomatic manifestations of AIDS can be relieved, enabling people to live to the full the remainder of their lives, and eventually achieve an easy death without the need for euthanasia.[30]

There are rare occasions when it is necessary to sedate a patient heavily in order to relieve intolerable distress in a patient whose dying is complicated by, for example, an agitated delirium or increasing obstruction of the windpipe. I am still bound, however, by the cardinal ethical principle that I must achieve my treatment goal with the least risk to the patient's life. In this case, rendering the patient unconscious is clearly less of an immediate risk than deliberately killing the patient. Those in favour of euthanasia may well say that I am splitting ethical and therapeutic hairs in as much as the endpoints of my action and that of the doctor who would actively assist death are identical. I disagree; for me there is a fundamental difference. Even in these extreme and rare circumstances, my intention is to alleviate suffering, not to shorten life. The practical, ethical and legal reality of this distinction has been upheld by the Report of the Select Committee on Medical Ethics.[17,31]

Further, my approach maintains a necessary measure of humility in the face of the mystery of life and death. The dangers of crossing the Rubicon are so great that, even though I may be forced by extreme circumstances to put one foot into the river, I will continue to respect the necessity of this ultimate barrier.[32,33,34,35]

Notes

1. Roy DJ, Rapin CH. Regarding euthanasia. European Journal of Palliative Care 1994; 1: 57–59.
2. World Health Organization. *Cancer Pain Relief.* Geneva: WHO, 1986.
3. Twycross RG. A doctor's dilemma. Journal of the CMF 1993; 39: 1–3.

4. Twycross R. A pain-free death? Christian Medical Quarterly 1993; February: 28–32.
5. Twycross R. *Relief of Pain in Far Advanced Cancer.* 2nd edn. Edinburgh: Churchill Livingstone, 1994.
6. Voluntary Euthanasia Society. *A Plea for Legislation to Permit Voluntary Euthanasia.* London: Headley Brothers Ltd, 1970.
7. Devlin P. *Easing the passing: The trial of Dr John Bodkin Adams.* London: The Bodley Head, 1985. pp 171–182.
8. Gillett G. Letting die, euthanasia and the Christian doctor. Journal of the CMF 1994; 40: 20–24.
9. Collins K, Gilhooly MLM, Murray K. Euthanasia: attitudes are influenced by age and religion. BMJ 1994; 309: 52.
10. Scott JF. Lamentation and euthanasia. Humane Medicine 1992; 8: 116–121.
11. Heintz APM. Euthanasia: can be part of good terminal care. BMJ 1994; 308: 1656.
12. van der Wal G, Diliman RJM. Euthanasia in the Netherlands. BMJ 1994: 308: 1346–1349.
13. Gunning KF. Euthanasia. Lancet 1991; 338: 1010–1011.
14. Commission on the Study of Medical Practice concerning Euthanasia. *Medical Decisions Concerning the End of Life (in Dutch).* The Hague: Staatsuitgeveri, 1991.
15. Keown J. Further reflections on euthanasia in the Netherlands in the light of the Remmelink Report and the van der Maas survey. In: Gormally L, (ed). *Euthanasia, Clinical Practice and the Law.* London: The Linacre Centre, 1994. pp 219–240.
16. Ward BJ, Tate PA. Attitudes among NHS doctors to requests for euthanasia. BMJ 1994; 308: 1332–1334.
17. House of Lords. *Report of the Select Committee on Medical Ethics.* HL Paper 21–1. London, HMSO, 1994.
18. Walton J. *Medical Ethics: Select Committee Report.* Hansard, May 9 1994. pp 1344–1349.

19. Alexander L. Medical science under dictatorship. N Engl J Med 1949; 241: 39–47.

20. Binding K, Hoche A. *The release of destruction of life devoid of value.* California: Life Quality, 1975. (Originally published in German by Felix Meiner, Leipzig, 1920).

21. Van der Maas PJ, Van Delden JJM, Pijnenborg L, Looman CWN. Euthanasia and other medical decisions concerning the end of life. Lancet 1991; 338: 669–674.

22. Smoker B. Remember the non-terminally ill and disabled. Voluntary Euthanasia Society Newsletter 1991; September: 10.

23. Spanjer M. Mental suffering as justification for euthanasia in the Netherlands. Lancet 1994; 343: 1630.

24. Fengisen R. A case against Dutch euthanasia. Hastings Center Report 1988; 19 (suppl): 22S–30S.

25. Twycross R. Where there is hope, there is life: a view from the hospice. In: Keown J, ed. *Examining Euthanasia: Legal, Ethical and Clinical Perspectives.* Cambridge: Cambridge University Press, 1995.

26. Zyliicz Z. The story behind the blank spot. American Journal of Hospice & Palliative Care 1993; 10: 30–34.

27. Bliss MR. Resources, the family and voluntary euthanasia. Br J Gen Pract 1990; 40: 117–122.

28. British Medical Association. *Euthanasia.* London BMA, 1988.

29. British Medical Association. Euthanasia. In: *Medical Ethics Today. Its Practice and Philosophy.* London: BMA, 1993. pp 175–179.

30. Fleming J. No final solution. Nursing Standard 1988; June 25: 11.

31. Walton J. The House of Lords on issues of life and death. J R Coll Physicians Lond 1994; 28: 235–236.

32. Gaylin W, Kass LR, Pellegrino ED, Siegier M. Doctors must not kill. JAMA 1988; 259: 2139–2140.

33. Vaux KL. Debbie's death: mercy killing and the good death. JAMA 1988; 259: 2140–2141.

34. Reichel W & Dyck AJ. Euthanasia: a contemporary moral quandary. Lancet 1989; ii: 1321–1323.
35. Roy DJ. Euthanasia: where to go after taking a stand? J Palliat Care 1990; 6: 3–5.

CHAPTER ELEVEN

GENETIC MANIPULATION

A. Caroline Berry

Dr Berry was Consultant Clinical Geneticist at Guy's Hospital from 1979 until her retirement in 1997. She served on the Board of Social Responsibility of the General Synod of the Church of England and chaired the Medical Study Group of the Christian Medical Fellowship. She has written extensively on the ethical aspects of genetics.

Introduction

What is genetic manipulation and how is it possible to manipulate our genes? The starting point was in 1953 when Watson and Crick suggested the structure of the molecule which is the fundamental stuff of life: deoxyribonucleic acid, usually abbreviated to DNA. It has the amazing capacity to be able to duplicate itself so that one molecule given the right conditions can become two identical molecules. More important was the discovery that this magic substance was in fact very simple. The molecule is made up of four chemicals called bases. These are adenine (A), thymine (T), guanine (G) and cytosine (C). The DNA molecule consists essentially of a string of these bases in varying order AATGCCTTATA etc. Each triplet of bases gives the signal or code for the manufacture of a certain

166

amino acid, e.g. AGA is the code for the amino acid arginine and a series of these amino acids are built up into a protein which the cell uses to develop itself or in energy transactions.

We now know that this genetic code is virtually the same in the simplest of organisms as it is in complex animals and in human beings. The code for the simplest of organisms such as a virus consists of a string of perhaps 200,000 bases GTTCGG . . . a printout that could be fitted onto a single sheet of A4 if the letters were small enough. At the other end of the scale we humans have 3,000 million letters (bases) in our code GTTCGGATATCG . . . so that the printout for the code for one individual would need the pages found in a thousand Bibles. Clearly we are more complex than a virus!

Each time a cell divides so that growth or repair can occur the entire sequence must be reproduced with absolute accuracy. An error, if in an important part of the sequence, will mean that the final product is faulty and disease may result. Many cancers arise because of errors accumulating as cells multiply over the course of a person's lifetime. Other errors may occur as the egg or sperm cells are produced and these will give rise to offspring with a genetic disease. Fortunately the body has over the millennia developed good surveillance and repair mechanisms so that many copying errors cause no damage. Most cells multiply safely and most children are born healthy.

We now know that ninety per cent of our human DNA appears not to have any active role and errors in this so-called 'junk DNA' do not have ill effects. We are still left with 30 million base pairs which code for every inherent characteristic of the person represented there. Already parts of the human genome have been sequenced, and the order of the individual base pairs is established for the entirety of some of the smaller genes, such as that coding for Factor IX, whose deficiency gives rise to Haemophilia B.

It can only be a matter of time before the entire human

genome is sequenced. The Human Genome Project is an international co-operative effort aiming to achieve this end, and vast sums of money are being poured into it, of the order of 200 million dollars per year world wide. If this continues it is likely to achieve its object by the turn of the century, and we will then know the 3,000 million combinations of the four bases (adenine, guanine, thymine and cytosine) which characterise the human make-up. Eventually, variations which lead to serious disease will be disentangled from variations with trivial or no effects, and each individual could be known by his or her characteristic unique sequence.

Manipulating our genetic make-up

How can we manipulate our genetic make-up? One of the amazing facts that emerged as our understanding increased is that since the code is the same throughout the plant and animal kingdoms it is possible to take a strip of DNA from one organism and insert it into another, and the new organism will process the imported DNA message as if it were its own. For example it is possible to take the gene (strip of DNA whose code gives the recipe) for human growth hormone. The hormone promotes growth in normal children and if missing the child's growth remains stunted until the hormone is supplied by injection. The growth hormone gene can be spliced into the much simpler genetic system of a bacterium. The bacterium responds to the new genetic information and starts to make the human growth hormone. By enabling the bacteria to multiply as is their habit, large quantities of human hormone can be harvested and used for treating children who lack the hormone. This pure 'engineered' hormone is a much safer product than that available previously. It had to be extracted from the brains of human corpses, a macabre source and not always a safe one as occasionally the brain contained the infectious virus for the dementia known as Creutzfeldt Jakob Disease, which years later may develop in the recipient.

It is this reciprocity of genetic information which is the foundation of genetic manipulation. The fact that a gene from one organism can be made to function in a very different one opens up dramatically far-reaching new possibilities. Some of these are entirely desirable while others have potential for both good and ill. As with any new and powerful technology it is very important that there is careful evaluation and forward thinking so that those who can benefit do so but major pitfalls and potential disasters are avoided.

Is genetic research ethical?

Is it right to pursue such research into the very fundamentals of our being? Some argue that such exploration of the human genetic make-up is presumptuous and that we are approaching too close to the essence of our humanity.

But our genetic code is the part of ourselves that we share with the rest of the biological world. Our genes are important building blocks but a person is more than the sum of their genes. The genes perhaps represent the dust of the earth into which, in the creation story in Genesis, God breathed and this made 'man' a living soul. We must not impart too great a value to our molecular blueprint. The capacity for faith and a propensity to sin are inherent but are not coded by our DNA. There is no prospect of gene manipulation giving us peace with God or love for our fellows.

Current use of molecular techniques in medicine

Genetic factors are important in the development of many common disorders such as asthma and diabetes, schizophrenia and epilepsy, but the link between genes and disease development is complex. Several genetic errors may be necessary before the disease manifests, or, more likely, genetic factors predispose an individual to develop the disease, but only if and when appropriate environmental influences come into play. For example, a person may have a genetic predisposition to obesity but will only become overweight if there is plenty of available food. This complex type of inheritance is exceedingly important because these conditions are common but the complexity means that molecular techniques are hard to apply and progress in this area is for future rather than present discussion.

Other rarer disorders depend entirely on the genetic make-up of an individual and it is with these so-called single gene disorders that current progress is being made. These disorders arise when a mutation (gene error) alters the function of a single gene so that the substance produced by that specific gene is faulty. They run in families in a predictable pattern according to the rules of Mendelian inheritance (dominant, recessive, X linked). Though individually rare, there are several thousand such diseases so that together they affect large numbers of people and, as they are often severe and at present most of them untreatable, they make a significant contribution to ill health in general. The genetic nature of the disease, often high recurrence risk and perhaps the need to inform other family members, adds to the burden of the family.

The finding of the error at the molecular level has useful implications for diagnosis but also increases our understanding of the underlying cause so that treatment can be approached in a rational way. For example, a mutation in a single gene on the X chromosome produces a condition known as Alport's syndrome, which affects the eye, the hearing and the kidney. It was puzzling to know why three such disparate organs were affected until it was discovered that the error is in a gene whose protein product is important in the development of each of these organs.

Identification of affected individuals and their carrier relatives

Although treatment is not yet possible, during the past decade suffering from diseases such as Duchenne muscular dystrophy have had major benefit from the new techniques. Identification of the specific mutation affecting that family may provide an accurate test for women wishing to know whether or not they carry the X-linked gene. For carriers, rapid and accurate prenatal testing can be done on a sample (chorion biopsy) obtained from the developing placenta at about ten weeks into a pregnancy. If the fetus is male and has the mutation, the pregnancy can be terminated.

Abortion is a contentious issue, although many people would accept its legitimacy for the avoidance of serious handicap, and the molecular techniques have made it possible to reduce the number of such abortions because they can be carried out on very much more precise grounds than previously. Ten years ago a girl with a brother with muscular dystrophy would have had an abortion simply because the fetus was shown to be a male, with perhaps a ten per cent chance of being affected. Nowadays such a girl would usually be able to continue her pregnancy unless an actual mutation, indicating a definitely affected male, was found to be present. Similar advances have occurred with many other single gene disorders.

Testing of healthy individuals: gene carriers

It is now becoming possible to test or screen healthy individuals to identify some of the genes they carry and the Nuffield Council on Bioethics has reviewed the ethical aspects of population screening.[1] Individuals may now be tested to see if they carry a gene that would predispose them to having a handicapped child in a future pregnancy. At present such testing is for recessively inherited genes so that a couple are only at risk of having an affected child if *both* carry the gene. An individual found to be a gene carrier need have no concerns about their own health but if their partner should also be a carrier they would have one chance in four of having an affected child in any pregnancy. The disorders tested for at present (thalassaemia, sickle cell disease, Tay Sachs disease and cystic fibrosis) are all severe and prenatal testing and abortion of affected fetuses is available. However, as treatment improves, the affected children do better and this has to be taken into account when abortion is considered.

Where family members are tested because there is already an affected individual known, the implications of the disease are reasonably clear for those tested. When random population testing is introduced very careful and truthful explanations are essential. There is considerable commercial interest in the development and promotion of this type of screening. It should be clear that it should only be introduced if adequate education and support are available.

Screening in relation to personal health

It is becoming possible to identify those whose genetic make up predisposes them to develop certain major diseases. For some, avoidance may be possible by change of life style (e.g. hypercholesterolaemia, a predisposition for fat deposition in the blood vessels leading to heart attack), change of occupation (e.g. alpha antitrypsin deficiency which predisposes to lung disease particularly with exposure to dust and smoke), or by early detection and treatment (some cancers). For others, such as Huntington's disease, which gives rise to dementia in early middle age, no such action is possible.

Screening: preventative action possible

In these circumstances testing seems eminently sensible and yet great care is necessary. People need to think carefully how they will cope with a positive test result. Will they be prepared to make the recommended changes in diet or habits if necessary? Will their life become so dominated by anxiety about the disease that they will regret knowing this aspect of the truth about themselves. Issues of life insurance, mortgages and employment need to be addressed. In an ideal world those at risk in some particular industrial environment should be employed elsewhere but when employment is scarce unjust discrimination may occur. Overall much must depend on the age of testing and the effectiveness of treatment or preventive measures for those at risk.

Screening: no preventative action possible

The adverse possibilities outlined above are all potential hazards without the benefits of possible prevention. At present screening of the population at large for such conditions seems valueless, but for those who know they are at high risk of inheriting the gene for, for example, Huntington's disease the possibility of testing gives those who want it an opportunity of knowing and planning their life accordingly. Again it is essential that each individual has the opportunity for careful consideration of how either result would affect them. For those who have lived for many years with the shadow of the disease looming over them finding that they are not at risk may be a mixed blessing. They are no longer different from other people and may find an important plank in the life they have built has disappeared. Christians know that God, who knows them from the time of conception, is fully aware of each person's genetic make-up and its implications. Now that it is starting to become possible for us to share in this knowing the important factor is how we use our increased self-knowledge.

Pre-implantation diagnosis

Further into the future but already being evaluated is pre-implantation diagnosis. At present a pregnant woman who has a test and is found to be carrying an abnormal child may be faced with deciding whether or not to have an abortion. This is very distressing for all concerned. Even Christians who accept abortion as a possible option see it as undesirable and disruptive, and to be avoided if alternative strategies are available. Indeed, the majority of those with no religious beliefs have similar views.

With pre-implantation diagnosis the pregnancy is started using *in vitro* (test tube baby) techniques. Several eggs are fertilised and then left to complete the first few cell divisions. When there are about eight cells present, one to two cells are removed and tested for the presence or absence of the mutated gene for which that pregnancy is known to be at risk (e.g. cystic fibrosis or Duchenne muscular dystrophy). Those shown not to have the mutation can then be returned to the mother's uterus and the pregnancy left to continue in the normal way. This technique is in the early stages of clinical use and as yet only a few hundred babies have been born, but initial results are encouraging.

Those Christians who believe that the human person, made in the image of God, is present from the moment that egg and sperm fuse would not countenance the dis-

174

carding of these pre-implantation embryos that are affected. Others, however, find this a far less disruptive procedure than abortion, though the 'hassle' of pregnancy initiated using these techniques must not be underestimated, even though with optimal management the likelihood of successful pregnancy is approaching that of natural conception.

Ethical aspects

The fact that such pre-implantation diagnosis is technically possible raises certain ethical concerns. Discarding pre-implantation embryos because they have a serious genetic error is one thing. But what should be the response to parents having the procedure done to exclude cystic fibrosis who say 'If there are several unaffected ones we would prefer the boys (or the girls) to be returned to the uterus.' Such double testing could be possible though at present most couples are more concerned about having a healthy child than one of the preferred sex. However, there must be a possibility that probes for other characteristics might be developed—height, athletic endurance or even perfect musical pitch. If such technology were available (which it is not), how would we view it?

The pre-implantation embryos concerned would all be the offspring of the parents and only genes already present in the parents would be identified so there is no question of manipulating the genes themselves. It would be a matter of choosing certain characteristics to be present rather than accepting the genetic lottery that currently arrives, cries and is placed lovingly in a crib. Is there morality in choosing uncertainty rather than investing one's talents (in this case genes) wisely?

Although the 'choice' scenario sounds exciting or alarming according to taste, it is likely to elicit from Christians a knee-jerk 'we must not play God'. However, at a pragmatic level it is difficult to see a serious demand. Most potential parents want their children to be happy and well adjusted rather than superbrats and for these attributes no single genes are likely to be responsible. Women have for years been able to opt for donor insemination with sperm from men of high IQ but few choose this; most babies will surely continue to be conceived in the usual way with only those with real problems using God's gifts of high technology.

The above discussion though should alert us to the broader concept of how much parents should choose and manipulate their children's characteristics as genetic engineering techniques are already having an impact here in a more subtle manner.

Production of human gene products

Using the genetic manipulation techniques described earlier a number of medicinally useful products are being manufactured. These include human insulin, growth hormone and a number of vaccines. The development of human growth hormone was particularly important as it coincided with withdrawal of the previously used substance extracted from the brains of the deceased (see above). Genetically engineered growth hormone is now generally available and being commercially promoted. It can promote growth not only in those who lack the natural hormone but also in normal children. Should parents of naturally short children request 'treatment' for their child? Paediatricians have differing views as much depends on whether or not being short is regarded as a disadvantage.

Being short or tall has little moral implication but how should parents respond if in the future other human gene products are discovered as the human genome project unfolds? What if brain growth promoters are discovered or muscle strength enhancers? It is because of the great commercial potential such developments could have that the current arguments about patenting are so vehement (see below). Again, though, we must remember that we already have access to anabolic steroids and mood-enhancing drugs and are having to live and legislate for the use of these. Are gene products very different to externally applied stimuli?

Gene therapy

We now need to consider more direct gene therapy. This was considered by a Department of Health Committee chaired by Sir Cecil Clothier[2] and their report and recommendations were published in 1992. Gene therapy may be either somatic or germline depending at what stage the manipulation is carried out.

Germline therapy involves manipulation of the ova and sperm or pre-implantation embryo. If an early embryo has its genetic constitution in any way altered then that alteration will affect all its cells including the germline and so its offspring will inherit the altered gene. Because of its possible impact on future offspring, the Clothier Committee recommended that this possibility should be set aside as a no-go area certainly for the time being. In reality the 'treatment' of embryos found to be genetically abnormal would be difficult and hazardous and a much more realistic option is simply to discard the abnormal embryos and return the unaffected ones to the uterus.

With *somatic cell* therapy the cells that are genetically manipulated are the patients non-reproductive somatic (body) cells, originating from bone marrow, skin or connective tissue. These are returned to the patient and circulate throughout the body. The chance of the germ cells in testis or ovary becoming altered is very remote. Thus the therapy would affect the person being treated but not his or her offspring.

Affected individuals with single gene disorders may be

treated by the replacement of the aberrant gene by a normal one in the hope that the normal gene product will be produced in the appropriate tissues. This is an exciting new area on the threshold of important advances. At the moment, the side effects of such treatment are unknown and the initial patients are those with serious untreatable disorders. The disease chosen for the first attempts at gene therapy is an immunological disorder, adenosine deaminase (ada) deficiency. The immune system of affected people is so incapacitated that the children live only a few years and, unless kept in isolation, they have continuing debilitating infections. Several children have been receiving regular infusions of their own blood cells which have been 'infected' with viral transporter which makes human ada; progress reports are encouraging.

There are major technical difficulties with this type of gene therapy. The gene must be inserted and must function in the appropriate cell. This is done by introducing the gene into a virus which is then made to infect the cell. Regulation of both the virus (so that it does not multiply and cause harm) and the amount of its protein that the gene produces, are both essential. As yet these are not always well understood and there is concern that malignant change might develop as time goes on.

While disorders involving cells such as those giving us immunity are readily accessible, diseases such as muscular dystrophy where the error affects muscle cells and cystic fibrosis where epithelial cells are involved provide further challenges. Efforts are being made to introduce genetically corrected cells into the respiratory epithelium of sufferers of cystic fibrosis.

Using a quite different approach, cells with genetically inserted markers are being used in cancer treatment, both to try to target the treatment to the appropriate cells and also to monitor the fate of cells injected with the aim of tumour destruction.

True somatic gene therapy is still very much in its infancy and progress is disappointingly slow. The ethical issues are chiefly those common to all novel treatment: the weighing of risks and possible benefits, ensuring that those being treated are fully informed and give their consent and that results can be assessed on properly collected data. In the United Kingdom any form of gene therapy can only be undertaken with the approval of the Gene Therapy Advisory Committee, which weighs up each proposal with regard to both its scientific and ethical aspects.

In 1996, at the instigation of the House of Commons Science and Technology Committee, the Human Genetics Advisory Commission was set up to monitor aspects of genetic technology relevant to the people of the United Kingdom.

Genetic manipulation in animals

There is much more scope for genetic manipulation in animals and plants than is remotely possible in humans. However, before considering this it is important to recognise how much animals have been 'genetically manipulated' over the millennia of domestication simply by controlled breeding. Mules, a sterile cross between horse and donkey, have been known since prehistoric times, and in the Book of Genesis Jacob managed to increase the number of speckled sheep in his uncle's flock and thus his own portion of inheritance. Racehorses are bred for fleetness of foot and thrive on it. Other results are more grotesque—turkeys whose breast muscles are so enlarged that they cannot mate and some of the more bizarre breeds of dog. We have accepted this natural genetic engineering without much thought. The modern techniques could speed such processes, giving cows with more or less creamy milk or leaner beef, but much of this has already been achieved by breeding.

The use of a *gene product* somewhat similar to the growth

hormone mentioned above has been used to increase milk yield but there is public concern about its safety so such milk is not produced in the UK. The cost to the cow and her owner is that her productive years are greatly reduced as her reserves are soon exhausted.

The chief ethical issues here are little different from those raised by factory farming with the benefits gained by cheap protein food being weighed against concern for animal welfare. The safety of the food products is a further essential concern discussed further below.

The use of genetically manipulated animals for medical research and gene product provision

It was mentioned earlier that certain important human products can be produced by inserting the appropriate DNA sequence into a bacterium. Some important products are too complex for a bacterium to handle and the problem is now being tackled by inserting the gene into an animal embryo so that it produces the required substance in the milk. The protein can be extracted from the milk, purified and used to treat human disease such as, for example, Haemophilia. This system seems little different ethically from using the animal for food or normal milk production.

More contentious is the production of animals, usually mice, who are 'tailor made' for certain research projects (transgenic animals). For example, it has been possible to make mice who have the gene for the human disease cystic fibrosis. The mice show some signs of the human disease and they can now be used to develop techniques for gene therapy and to further understanding of the human disease. 'Onco mouse' has been manipulated so that each mouse is prone to develop early cancer and so again can be used to research new treatments and preventive methods. People question the morality of breeding animals destined to be sick but the use of such creatures means that overall answers are likely to be obtained using fewer animals than would previously have been possible and of course for many diseases this approach saves patients from acting as the earliest guinea pigs.

Christians have a double responsibility in all these areas. There is the need to promote the health and welfare of those belonging to our human community, in particular those who are sick or potentially undernourished. On the other hand as stewards of God's creation we have a responsibility to members of the animal kingdom. Maintaining this tension is difficult as inevitably different groups within the community have differing priorities but with all these situations it is essential to balance the expected gain from the research with the expected suffering of the animal, a principle that applies as much to more ordinary research.

Genetic manipulation and the environment

Here again we have to balance likely benefits and possible risks. Genetically engineered organisms (GEOs) can be tailor made for certain functions such as to control pests or to counter pollution including oil spills. Yet there is natural anxiety about the release of such organisms for fear that once out in the natural world they might behave in a bizarre or unexpected way and give rise to an environmental disaster greater than the one they were used to avert. Ever since the power and versatility of the molecular techniques became apparent, scientists have been concerned about the possibility of escape and uncontrolled multiplication of an organism genetically manipulated in the laboratory. Initial fears were so great that in 1974 an international moratorium on this work was proposed by Paul Berg of Stanford University and other members of the United States National Academy of Sciences. Leading scientists from countries throughout the world united in an unprecedented manner and experiments ceased while researchers focused on the mechanisms and scope of these techniques and steps that could be taken to minimize the risk of a disastrous accident.

At the same time the United Kingdom had a somewhat different approach to the problem. A Working Party of the Advisory Board for the Research Councils was set up to study the Experimental Manipulation of the Genetic Composition of Micro-organisms. It was chaired by Lord Ashby and reported in 1975.[3] This group saw the handling of genetically engineered organisms as essentially no different from the handling of highly pathogenic organisms like smallpox virus. They did not suggest a moratorium but recommended that experiments should be carried out with stringent 'containment' facilities. These recommendations have now been expanded and built into a legal framework alongside other health and safety regulations. Similar safeguards were adopted by other countries and the Berg moratorium was lifted. Its existence, however, showed that it is possible for scientists to work together in a responsible manner foregoing exciting new research because of the risk of harm to the population as a whole.

New developments continue to arise so that constant vigilance is essential. In 1989 the Royal Commission on Environmental Pollution published its thirteenth report.[4] This was a comprehensive study, including topics such as the release of genetically engineered viruses to control caterpillar pests which damage crops of cabbages and the improvement of soya bean growth in rural Africa by inoculating seeds with a bacterium which enhances nitrogen fixation. These techniques could be important in improving world food supplies but, as the commission spells out, there are as yet many uncertainties and these rightly must be a cause for concern. Specific anxieties include:

(a) There is little information available on the behaviour of GEOs in the environment.

(b) Unlike chemicals, biological agents can multiply in the environment. There is therefore a risk that once released it will be impossible to control them. This may be especially the case with micro-organisms and viruses rather than with larger animals which are relatively easily detected and contained.

(c) Gene transfer between microbes, plants and animals does occur naturally and introduced genes may function in some unknown way if transferred in the environment to a new organism.

In view of this the Commission recommended that the current voluntary controls should be superseded by statutory controls with comprehensive legislation. While seeing no need for any moratorium on the use of GEOs they stressed that all releases of such organisms should be subject to licensing by the Secretary of State and that all licence proposals should be scrutinised by well-informed experts. This should ensure that risks to the environment were minimised by the use of appropriate available precautions. Careful monitoring of the environmental impact should be mandatory.

The Commission's report is comprehensive and provides a useful review of the technology and its applications together with the potential hazards and suggestions as to how these may be at least minimised. Here again we have a tool with great potential for good if wisely and responsibly used but which, if allowed untrammelled development simply according to market forces or scientific curiosity, could do unpredictable harm.

Genetic manipulation and agriculture

The insertion of new genetic information into plants probably has the most far reaching and significant potential with effects likely in the foreseeable future. By appropriate techniques it is possible to introduce novel features into established crop plants. The possibility of unsquashable tomatoes has caught the public imagination, but the insertion of genes into appropriate plants for frost or drought resistance, pest resistance and ability to grow on poor or salty soils has great potential for improving the world's food supply but yet also has major implications for world trade. The impact on the West Indian economy if genetically manipulated bananas could be grown in Watford is not hard to work out.

Genetic manipulation could potentially resolve the world's food and energy crises and research should therefore be encouraged but it brings with it serious implications for economic destabilisation and profiteering by the rich countries at the expense of the needy.

The general public tends to be chiefly concerned about safety aspects and since the provision of safe food and water supplies must be a major concern of government legislation this needs high priority. Perhaps foodstuffs produced by these techniques should be subjected to the same stringent licensing procedures as are new drugs. As Christians, however, our chief concern must be that justice is done and that the interests of the poorer and weaker nations are protected.

Patenting

It is clear from what has gone before that enormous commercial implications are inherent in each new molecular discovery. To whom do the newly identified tiny strips of DNA belong? Proposals so far include:

(a) to the person or group who unravelled the sequence;
(b) to who or whatever provided the cells from which the sequence was discovered;
(c) to God who 'invented' the code in the first place and has known each sequence since the beginning of time.

Companies have attempted to patent minute segments of DNA as they isolate them and before anything is known of their function, although patent law includes usefulness among the essential criteria for patent granting. The issue is a live one in the law courts and the European Commission is drawing up legislation. In November 1994 the British High Court ruled that a Californian biotechnology company, Chiron Corporation, effectively owned the sequence for the Hepatitis C virus. Two rival companies were judged to have breached patents when making and marketing their own test kits for the detection of the virus.

The scientific community is concerned that research findings will no longer be freely published because those who discover new sequences will be bound by industrial secrecy. Even when findings are published, workers wanting to make use of this information are being charged royalties so that diagnostic tests become increasingly expensive.

Drug companies and other commercial organisations do, however, need to be able to recoup their huge investment in developing new products and the patent system is at present the only means available. In responding to criticism the Vice-President of the Chiron Corporation stated that 'safeguarding these rewards is vital if future advances in health-care are to be achieved'.

In 1993 the four groups involved in the provision of Genetic Testing and Counselling for the National Health Service in the United Kingdom issued a joint statement stating why they were in principle against the granting of patents on human gene sequences. In particular the patenting of sequences before their function was known seemed in contradiction to the 'usefulness' criterion. The group proposed that patenting should be limited to new developments by which known sequences could be made useable in, for example, gene therapy or a new diagnostic test. The patent would apply to the new technique or delivery system rather than to the sequence of the gene being used.

It may well be that this whole arena is so complex that a new approach will be necessary and new systems devised by which companies' investment can be rewarded without research and patients being adversely affected.

Conclusions

In its submission to the Clothier Committee, the Board of Mission of the Church in Wales wrote: 'As Christians, we are aware of the awesome responsibilities of human beings as made in the image and likeness of God, and with authority under God over the whole created order; but we are also aware that humanity is part of God's creation, sharing solidarity with it, and responsible to God for the proper stewardship of what is entrusted to us. We must exercise a proper humility before the structures of human life and in the use which is made of knowledge gained concerning the human genome.'

The technology of genetic manipulation is an immensely powerful God given tool which we can use for the relief of suffering and to help overcome some of the problems that beset our overcrowded world. We have, however, to remember that the men of old displayed their technical superiority by building the Tower of Babel in a spirit of pride and self-sufficiency. We need a spirit of wisdom to enable us to exercise responsible stewardship in an attitude of dependence on God so that the benefits are harnessed while the weak, the vulnerable and the environment are protected.

Notes

1. Nuffield Council for Bioethics. *Genetic Screening: Ethical Issues*. London: Nuffield Council on Bioethics, 1993.
2. Report of the Committee on the Ethics of Gene Therapy. London: HMSO, 1992.
3. Report of the Working Party on the Experimental

Manipulation of the Genetic Composition of Micro-organisms. London: HMSO, 1975.

4. Royal Commission on Environmental Pollution, 13th Report. *The Release of Genetically Engineered Organisms to the Environment.* London: HMSO, 1989.

CHAPTER TWELVE

PORNOGRAPHY—PAST, PRESENT AND FUTURE

Claire Wilson-Thomas

Claire Wilson-Thomas works in the Public Policy Department at Christian Action, Research and Education (CARE). She has contributed substantially to analysing the impact of pornography on personal and national life for both adults and children.

Pornography is all about sex and money. The pornography business involves thousands of people, from the corner newsagent selling a few magazines to multi-million pound empires producing and distributing material world-wide. Pornography has gained a cloak of acceptance in our society because so many people are involved. Yet its impact is equally wide from regular users of sex establishments in Soho to children exchanging disks in the school playground.

Sex was God's idea

Why should we be concerned about pornography? Because pornography undermines sex as God intended. God created men, women and sex. 'God saw all that he had made, and it was very good.'[1] The Bible is very honest about sexual relationships, and tells us three important things:

(a) Sex cannot be separated from marriage;
(b) Children are the natural (though not inevitable) consequence of a sexual relationship;
(c) The sexual relationship is joyful—nowhere in the Bible
is a negative view presented of sex within marriage.

Pornography undermines these messages.

What is pornography?

The word pornography comes from the Greek and literally means 'the writing of [or about] whores'. It is
generally accepted to cover a wide range of materials
from 'top-shelf' magazines like *Playboy* and *Penthouse*,
portraying women as inviting and wanting sexual activity
in many different situations and poses, to acts of great
violence and cruelty involving women, children and in
some cases men. The distinction between so-called 'hard',
and 'soft' pornography is subjective rather than legal. A
useful and simple description of pornography was coined
in 1972 by the Longford Committee: 'That which
exploits and dehumanises sex so that human beings are
treated as things, and women, in particular as sex
objects.'[2]

How does pornography portray women?

Pornographic material depicts women as a mere assemblage
of physical parts with particular emphasis on the breasts and
genitalia. There is little or no attempt to show the other
aspects and strengths of a woman's character as a mental or
spiritual being.

How does pornography show the sexual relationship?

Invariably pornography portrays sexual intercourse as the
only aspect of a relationship between men and women. It
rarely, if ever, shows the sexual relationship in the loving,

caring context of marriage. The message is sex is available wherever you want it, whenever you want it and in whatever form you want it. Pornography is about consumption rather than giving.

What is the purpose of pornography?

Medical textbooks and manuals designed to improve sexual technique can have explicit sexual content without being pornographic. By contrast, pornography is not designed with an educational purpose. Its objective is to titillate, stimulate and provoke sexual desire.

What about page 3?

If the above tests are applied to the pictures regularly appearing in *The Sun* and *The Sport*, they can rightly be defined as pornographic. Although such photographs do not show explicit sexual activity, they do fail the test of treating women as more than mere physical beings. The brief accompanying text usually also has some titillating overtone.

The issue of censorship

Censorship has become something of a sacred cow for libertarians. In fact it is something that we all do every day of our lives. We are constantly faced with decisions of where to draw the line. Are those against censorship really arguing that there should be no line at all? Are they arguing that child pornography and violent material should be allowed? No, the true subject of debate is where the line should be drawn and by what process that decision is reached. It needs to be informed by academic research and by the testimonies of those who are and have been involved, directly or indirectly, with pornography.

Is pornography a bit of harmless fun?

This is a question that has been the subject of debate for many years. The evidence of those who have been addicted to pornography, those who have suffered as victims, those who work with sexual offenders and research conducted in academic studies suggests that pornography does have serious negative effects to which society must respond.

Harmful effects of pornography

The availability of pornography and its consumption by men contribute to a lowering of the general attitude towards women and a belief that they are sexually available.

Pornography promotes the idea of constant and complete sexual satisfaction without love and commitment. It can promote destructive fantasy and can damage the ability of men to have a proper sexual relationship thereby ruining the mutual love and respect which should characterise sex within marriage.

The testimonies of sex offenders and those working with them clearly show that pornography does contribute to the development of a pattern of sexual crime. When detectives raided the home of a recently convicted child murderer, 'a vast collection' of paedophiliac material, including books, videos and magazines, was uncovered.[3]

Pornography is used directly by some offenders to 'soften up' victims, and describes sexual activity that is subsequently copied in sex crimes. The saddest cases are those involving children.

The changing nature of pornography

Pornography is found in many different types of media: newspapers, books, magazines, comics, films, videos, television, telephones and computers. It can be easily purchased from an ordinary shop, a licensed sex shop, by mail order or through new technology such as the Internet.

Magazines are often the start of an individual's involvement with pornography. Evidence suggests that the number of titles available has increased in recent years, and that the material they contain has become more explicit.

The major new avenue for pornographers over the last five years has been computers. The main differences between computer pornography and that on other media are:

(a) images can easily be altered by the user, e.g. to put a child's head on an adult's body;
(b) often the pornography is interactive, that is the user makes decisions about the pose of the women, what she is wearing etc.;
(c) computer images can be reproduced as a perfect copy each time, so the quality of the media never deteriorates;
(d) pictures of photographic quality can be reproduced on local printers;
(e) vast numbers of images can be transferred across the world in seconds.

One of the biggest concerns over the rapid rise of computer pornography is its impact on children's development—and their safety. Early reports suggested that computer discs with *Playboy* type images were circulating in primary school playgrounds. Several years on, the concern of parents and teachers is the nature of the material children are accessing on the Internet, a computer library of extensive educational value. Unfortunately, it is also a source of hardcore pornography. Young children are unlikely to have the means of coping with these pornographic images.

The Internet allows pornography to be available night and day to everyone with a computer connection. A child or adult at their home/school/office desk can easily and quite secretly obtain large quantities of the more extreme and violent hardcore pornography, which they would normally have to go specifically looking for, and which in the past children are unlikely to have seen. To have this range of material available at the press of a button is a new scenario.

Evidence suggests that individuals, especially children and teenagers, can become 'addicted' to using computers. The mixture of the addictive nature of pornography with the addictive nature of the technology is potentially very dangerous. It could produce long-term effects in terms of damage to young men, teenagers and children and their image of sexuality and women, and could lead to an increasing amount of sexual activity at an early age. It is logical to suppose that if young children are seeing *Playboy* images or worse *now*, a percentage will become addicted to hard core material before they leave full-time education.

In addition, interactive computer pornography offers the user the opportunity to exercise control directly over their experience, unlike any other form of pornography. This element of control and dominance is a feature often associated with sexual crime. The sexual crime that stirs up the strongest feeling is that involving children.

The growth of the Internet as a means of global communication has been phenomenal, and is continuing. With it have come many benefits and also difficult questions, particularly on the nature of adult and child pornography, and how to restrict children's access without restricting 'free speech'. The worldwide distribution of child pornography—a permanent record of child abuse—has become obvious and calls for action have been loud and vigorous. A solution requires the co-operation of the whole international community.

Future trends

We are likely to see an increase in interactive technology over the next few years, culminating with virtual reality, an incredible use of technology with head-set and gloves that allows what you see and feel to seem virtually real. Of course all these technologies can be used for good: education, bomb disposal, remote medical surgery. However, leading software manufacturers say that sex will be one of the big applications driving the development of the interactive CD-ROM industry, dangling the carrot of safe sex. Another speculates that big changes in 'virtual reality' will occur when programmes start being written 'directly for the brain'. Primitive 'virtual reality' suits are already available, and estimates vary as to how soon these suits will reach the market. The challenge facing us is how to regulate these new technologies to harness the good but reduce the possibility for abuse.

Responding-law and enforcement

The law

There is a 'patchwork quilt' of legal provisions in England and Wales that touch on some aspects of pornography. Scotland and Northern Ireland share some of these provisions but also have separate and distinctive statutes. Over this 'patchwork quilt' there is a single blanket law (in England and Wales) defining what is acceptable in terms of content of any media: the 1959 Obscene Publications Act. This is the most significant Act which urgently needs amendment.

In section 1, the Act defines an article as obscene if 'its effect . . . is such as to tend to deprave and corrupt persons who are likely, having regard to all relevant circumstances, to read, see or hear the matter contained or embodied in it'. It is this definition of obscenity—not a definition of pornography—which has been the subject of debate for many years. There is general consensus that it is not easy to understand or apply. In 1959, Mr Justice Byrne said, 'Deprave and corrupt means to be morally bad, to pervert, or to debase and corrupt morally. It is extremely difficult to prove this.' A jury has to consider the impact of the material on the person, and the likely audience or readership of the material. Lawyers concentrate on the immediate audience for the material, but ignore who may see it later, e.g. videos seen at home by children for whom they are not intended.

The Act makes it an offence to publish an obscene article, whether for gain or not, or to have an obscene article for publication for gain. Publish here means to distribute, circulate, sell, let on hire, give or lend, or the transmission of obscene material by electronic means. It is important to remember that is not an offence to possess indecent or obscene material unless it portrays children.

Material that would otherwise be defined as obscene can be published for the public good if the material is 'in the interest of science, literature, art or learning, or other objects of general concern'. While this provision is not unreasonable, it is often exploited by lawyers, for instance by suggesting that pornographic magazines have therapeutic value for sex offenders.

Penalties

There are two possible penalties under the Obscene Publications Act. The first is under Section 2 and involves trial by magistrate or jury and on conviction a fine or imprisonment. Section 2 is only used by the police in the case of the most extreme material. The trials are long and costly with no certainty of success because of the vagueness of the definition of obscenity and the loopholes it provides.

Under Section 3 the police are allowed to seize and forfeit obscene material, but the individual selling or distributing it is not penalised personally other than by losing the stock. This offence is easier to implement and is less costly in police and court time, but it lacks real bite. Often the forfeited stock is replaced by new material within hours. During 1994, offences under Section 2 of the Act were classified as serious arrestable offences, which created new police powers of search and seizure and a new power of arrest for obscenity and child pornography offences.

Reform of the law

Various attempts have been made to reform the Obscene Publications Act, but with little success. They have been based on different formulas: altering the 'tendency to deprave and corrupt' test to 'grossly offensive to a reasonable person', linking this with the manner in which the material deals with a list of violent or sexual acts. Others have tried to define obscenity by a list of activities that may be considered obscene.

Clearly a change in the law is needed, but a new law has to be consistent with the traditions of the British legal system, be easily understood and be enforceable. The Conservative Government of 1992–97 was unwilling to put forward a new alternative itself as it considered obscenity a matter of personal choice. Although the Conservative Government repeatedly stated that if a back-bencher were to put forward a law that would improve on the current position they would offer support, they did not consider any of the proposals worth while pursuing.

Enforcement

Despite the multi-million pound and international nature of the pornography industry there are few specialist police squads dealing with obscenity offences in the UK. The Metropolitan Police's Paedophile and Child Pornography Unit (formerly the Obscene Publications Branch) has a national and international reputation for investigating child pornography and paedophile rings. A small number of police forces have developed expertise in computer pornography. The Metropolitan Police Clubs and Vice Unit investigates adult pornography offences.

Computer pornography is the door to a whole new generation of technologies upon which pornography will flourish. It is therefore essential that adequate control and enforcement are in place, not only in the UK, but in Europe and around the World. Whilst there is still much debate about how to tackle the difficult legal and enforcement issues posed by the international nature of the Internet, there is co-operation between international law enforcement agencies, and information is regularly passed to police forces at home and abroad by the UK's Internet Watch Foundation, set up in 1996 to combat child pornography on the Internet.

Behind all the technicalities of enforcement in the UK there has to be an adequate deterrent to stop pornographers producing this material. Most action under the Obscene Publications Act does not lead to personal fines or imprisonment. In Customs cases, if a case does go to court, they receive a small fine that can be easily recouped in a short time from the lucrative sales of pornographic material.

Our response

Can we make a difference? Individually and collectively, yes. We need to cultivate an attitude of non-acceptance. When public opinion became concerned about the amount of violence on videos, the law was changed. We need to ensure we are not being 'conformed to the world',[5] but are being transformed by the renewing of our minds. This does not mean a 'holier-than-thou' attitude of self-righteousness, but a concern to persuade others not to accept pornography. Positive action to present sexual relationships in the proper context plays a vital role in campaigning against pornography. We should also not just campaign against what is bad, but applaud what is good. We should support newsagents who do not stock pornography. We should write to TV and radio producers commending the programmes we enjoy that do not include smut and sexual innuendo.

Increasingly we need to be aware of the possible availability of pornography to our children. Parents need to appreciate its impact and be vigilant in monitoring what children see on videos, video games and home computers.[6]

Conclusions

Pornography and those that produce it must be challenged. Pornography has many victims: children, those involved in sexual attacks, women in relationships with those addicted to pornography, and the addicts themselves. Most importantly, we must see beyond the printed page to the underlying forces of pornography. We must counter the false imagery conveyed in pornography and combat it with truth.

Notes

1. Genesis 1:31.
2. Longford Committee 1972.
3. The case of Robert Black is described in detail in: Wyre R and Tate T. *The Murder of Childhood*. London: Penguin, 1995.
4. Merchant V. *Computer Pornography in Schools*. University of Central Lancashire, 1994.
5. Romans 12:2.
6. For practical suggestions see: Wilson-Thomas C, Williams N. *Laid Bare, A Path through the Pornography Maze*. London: Hodder and Stoughton, 1996.

Further reading

Williams N. *False Images: Telling the Truth about Pornography*. Eastbourne: Kingsway, 1991.

CHAPTER THIRTEEN

SUBSTANCE ABUSE

Duncan Vere

Professor Vere is Emeritus Professor of Therapeutics in the University of London and Consulting Physician to the Royal London Hospital. He has contributed to the literature not only on clinical pharmacology and therapeutics and substance abuse but also on the ethical aspects of medicine generally.

'Substance abuse' implies the taking of materials for pleasure, adventure or other such gain in ways which often damage the user or those around them. This abuse may be intermittent or regular. The fact that it has become abuse is often apparent largely to outside observers, less to the misusers themselves. Single uses of potentially hazardous drugs as a gesture are not included in this description; they are called 'parasuicide' or 'deliberate self harm'. What substances may be so abused? They include food, drinks such as alcohol, drugs and other remedies and tobacco.

Why abuse?

What properties, if any, do these substances have in common? They are all materials which seem to satisfy a perceived need or appetite. They also cause damage which is not at first perceptible, even after a long delay. So they are 'please now, pay later' materials. What are the desires that abused substances may be taken to satisfy? Clearly some are programmed into all of us: urges towards satisfying hunger, sex, social recognition and possessiveness. There are also self-esteem, the desire to signify, the urge to experience alternatives to established social norms or simply to experience life in some new way. There is also the desire to escape from the humdrum, the threatening or the fearful.

But the problem with some drugs is that they can induce a desire to take them which supplants or provides alternatives to these ordinary pre-programmed desires within us. They do this by depressing some bodily perception (e.g. hunger, pain) so that if they are then discontinued a 'rebound' occurs, increasing the sensation which they had suppressed, so leading to a severe craving for the substance again. A state of dependence, whether psychological or physical or both has ensued such that stopping drug use evokes unpleasant symptoms which can be relieved only by resuming its use.

Many of the features which may predispose to drug abuse have been recognised for some years; other suspected factors have been discounted, some remain to be discovered. A painstaking survey by the Home Office disclosed no evidence for a characteristic personality among drug misusers.[1] In addition, those with much experience of drug and alcohol abusers seem to agree that the most frequently observed antecedent of drug dependence is a deep hurt or rejection, whether actual or just perceived, often in childhood.[2]

Abused substances

What substances are used in these ways? Across the world they are many indeed, but the substances which most commonly induce characteristic dependence states in Britain include opiates and synthetic opioids such as morphine, diamorphine (heroin), codeine and dextropropoxyphene (a weak opioid in co-proxamol or 'Distalgesic' tablets), cocaine and free cocaine base ('crack'), nicotine, alcohol, sedatives and tranquillisers. Drugs which induce dependence weakly, but can also damage, include those which are taken intermittently to expand perception such as cannabis, lysergide (LSD), toadstool and cactus-derived drugs like mescaline, solvent fumes, amphetamines and the like including 'designer drugs' of rave parties such as 'Ecstasy' and pseudoephedrine.

Factors in abuse

Many damaging uses of substances are part of risk-taking behaviour, the gain being exhilaration or social superiority, especially where it had been perceived as lacking. This use is similar to some forms of high-risk motor racing, mountain climbing or stunt aviation, without the skills or sporting pleasures which are parts of these. Peer rivalry and emulation, especially in teenagers, are kindred motivations.

Are these varied abuses all disparate, or are there common biochemical and psychological threads which unite them? The latter seems to be the case.[3] Studies in London[4] and Birmingham[5] in the 1960s showed that as each town gained its first heroin abusers, their numbers rose quite rapidly. But the rate of growth tailed off once a fraction of the young population had started to use the drug. It appeared that within the juvenile sector there was a saturable sub-population of susceptibles. This was not an absolutely defined but a graded sub-population; areas with the greatest availability of heroin also had a higher susceptible population than others.

Similar evidence for alcohol was given by the Scottish Home and Health Department.[6] Whisky consumption was a remarkably constant function of available per capita income, not as such, but in terms of its purchasing power for whisky, as the price varied, and the same was true for hospital admissions for alcohol related diseases. The late Sir William Paton[7] showed, from very diverse populations, including the US armed forces, that patterns of drug taking were remarkably similar for opiates, alcohol and cannabis; a relative susceptibility gradient for drug taking, which moved up or down with drug availability and social context, but where the basic pattern was strikingly of the same shape whatever the population or drug involved.

Thus, simply to regard the substances as the problem is entirely naive; the personal factors within those who abuse them must be at least as important as the substances themselves. Food is necessary and its use universal, but to blame food entirely for the obesity of a bulimic person would clearly be absurd; so it is with drugs. Drug-dependent people are notoriously unable to say why they behave as they do, but one can recollect one or two intelligent people who explained that they had in fact been seeking a chemical 'prop' for years before they took heroin. They began with car fuel, glue solvents, tobacco with or without cannabis, alcohol. But none of these 'satisfied' them, so they went on to 'hard' drugs. This is not to say that the 'soft' drugs 'lead to escalation' to the 'hard', but rather that nothing satisfied an emotional craving which drove them on.

It is clear that there is no characteristic pattern of the 'drug abusing person'.[1] Anyone may choose such satisfactions, though susceptibility varies depending upon resistive factors within the person and substance availability about them.

What then are the factors within or around someone which may impel them towards such fulfilments and away from the normal goals and satisfactions of healthy living? Low self-esteem and a feeling of social rejection, whether real or imagined, seem to play a part. Many dependent persons will date their habit back to a shocking life event such as the sudden loss of a loved partner or a marriage break-up. But great care is needed to cross-check such claims since these people often blame such events for the habit, when others affirm that the event occurred because their habit had triggered it. Social ambitions are linked to rejection; a longing to opt out of ordinary society and to opt into the appreciative reception of an alternative set of people who share a drug habit. This partly explains the social rituals associated with many substance habits; these are nowhere more obvious than with alcohol and tobacco.

More recently, biochemical evidence has accumulated[8,9] which indicates that alcohol-dependent animals produce brain chemicals from the breakdown of the drug which resemble opiate molecules. There may be a common biochemical mechanism involved in dependence. This could account for some striking similarities in dependence behaviour with, for example, barbiturates and alcohol and also the ready conversion from one drug to the other when supplies fail.

Social cost of abuse

What can be the social context of these problems? The cost of substance abuse to the nation is colossal. The most direct problems of crime, accident and disease invoked by it are clear enough. Much serious crime is conducted under the influence of alcohol and much juvenile crime is done to gain the money to buy drugs. The desire to gain abused drugs damages people in many ways, but none is clearer than the disordered social behaviour associated with it. The altered perception of an addicted person dissociates their desired goals, emotional satisfaction and the obtaining of their drug from all else. Life is centred upon it. Work and relationships are destroyed unless they collude with drug possession. Life becomes an acted lie in which everything becomes true or false solely in relation to drug possession. Their testimony cannot be trusted.

Inevitably addicts will have to fund their habit through dishonest means. For heroin abuse it is necessary to gain up to eighty pounds a day, an appetite which can be satisfied only through crime, deceit, often prostitution. But the ill effects of the habit frustrate the opportunities so gained as the abuser spends ever longer periods in hospital or in prison. And the illegal drug traffic which supplies these abusers involves yet more crime and violence. This trade flourishes not simply because it is illegal but because it is highly profitable, a market force which sucks into itself major national resources needed for other uses. In other countries where drug legislation is absent or ineffective this includes agricultural land given over to drug production and the marked loss of industrial profitability arising from a drugged work-force. The money needed to gain drugs will always exceed the natural resources of a drug abuser, even of the very wealthy; this can be the case even for alcohol. The effects upon family life are highly destructive.[10]

Magnitude of abuse

What are the costs to the nation of substance abuse? Every year some 14,000 young people die from drug abuse[11] and a quarter of burglaries, half of deaths from fire and one third of drownings are related to it. By the age of fifteen, ten per cent smoke, nearly twenty per cent use cannabis, five per cent psychedelics and one per cent diamorphine.[12]

New addict notifications have risen steadily in the United Kingdom over the last twenty years for heroin, methadone and cocaine. This rise is sixteen-fold for heroin and seven-fold for both methadone (used to substitute for heroin) and for cocaine.[13] But it is clear that notified addicts are only a fraction of the real total. From these facts alone it is also clear that drug dependence centres do not contain the problem, indeed they are probably multiplying it to some degree by providing a legal source of drugs in addition to the illegal sources used by the same addicted persons. Drug withdrawal programmes work only for those who want continuously to leave their habit; this is only some five per cent to ten per cent of carefully chosen persons, selected for their evident motivation.[14] Even when a strong stimulus to indicate drug withdrawal such as a successful outcome of pregnancy happens, some 76 per cent of mothers remain addicted after one year.[15]

Currently, some thirty-eight per cent smoke, and this contrasts with comparable figures for 1972 of forty-five per cent smokers.[13] Despite some improvement (a fall from thirty-seven per cent in 1982 to thirty-one per cent in 1990) in the figures for male nicotine consumption, that by females has remained much the same (thirty-two per cent to twenty-eight per cent) and has begun to rise since 1990 despite Government 'health warnings'.[16,17] One- sixth of all deaths are tobacco related.[16]

Alcohol presents a more complex but still disturbing picture. There was a remarkable increase in alcohol-related illnesses between 1971 and 1975; hospital admissions nearly doubled for men and more than doubled for women.[18] Alcohol consumption peaked in 1979, fell until 1982, and then slowly rose again till 1992[19] when some twenty-seven per cent of males and twelve per cent of females were drinking over safe limits. There is a direct linear relationship between alcohol-related mortality and per capita consumption per year; in 1981 the United Kingdom compared favourably with most European and North American nations[20] but that situation has changed. The level of alcohol consumption in males had fallen to 6.2 litres (as pure alcohol) per year in 1981, but rose again by 1989 to 7.2 litres, an increase which would lead to the expectation that cirrhosis mortality would increase to 1.5 times the level of 1981. The per capita consumption doubled between the years 1949 and 1979[21] and during those years cirrhotic deaths also doubled.[22,23] The Chief Medical Officer's Report in 1994 revealed that 35,000 young people under fifteen years of age are drinking more than the 'safe limit' for alcohol.

Deaths from volatile substance abuse have risen steadily from 8 per annum in 1976 to 150 per annum in 1990.[24]

Controlling abuse

What is being done to control and to combat this growing problem? Some attention is paid to prevention. Evidence by the Royal College of Physicians[25] to the Social Services Committee of the House of Commons stressed prevention, emphasising that there was a sharp limit to what the medical profession could achieve since the roots of the problem seemed to be 'social' and 'economic'. The Advisory Committee on Alcoholism[26] discussed the two main avenues open to further prevention, education and restricting availability, recommending that the latter should not be relaxed whereas the former should be strengthened. Both abstention and abolition were regarded as unattainable, since they would never 'command broad approval from society'.

The aim was, therefore, to encourage moderate drinking. Part of the recommended education was 'to educate the young for responsible living'. It recommended that licensing hours should not be extended, noting that their reduction in 1914–1918 had curtailed drunkenness convictions and liver cirrhosis. The Commissioner of Metropolitan Police laid great stress upon education as a preventive measure to reduce drug demands.[27]

A similar debate has proceeded over nicotine, where the tobacco industry has suppressed the publication of evidence for its addictive potential,[28] while adjusting nicotine levels in tobacco so that addiction to them is likely to accrue.

But what has in fact happened? Despite all the official advice, funding for support agencies for young drug dependants has been reduced; tobacco and alcohol advertising to the young has never been curtailed effectively.[29] The available alcohol has been increased by the Licensing (Amendment) Bill of 1976 and again in 1988, against all the evidence to the contrary presented in parliamentary debate. It has been argued from two surveys (in 1987 and 1989) designed to straddle the year when licensing hours were again lengthened that no increase in alcohol consumption resulted. If there has been education, it has not worked effectively. Young people have been shown to misunderstand all of the most salient features about drugs of dependence; the most important source of their information are television and peer sharing.[30]

Treatment of addicted persons and containment of their social problems is of some, albeit insufficient, value. Despite the poor results from containment and therapy discussed above, their outcome seems better than what is found in cities which have not supported those policies, such as Glasgow.[31]

In summary, the generally acknowledged principles for containment and for prevention are to restrict availability, prevent advertisement, to educate the young and to provide counsel for those (a majority) of dependent persons who find their habit uncontrollable but wish to be released from it. Current policies, by contrast, emphasise punishment despite the fact that prisons and detention centres are known to be among the most effective sites of drug proselytism. Education from outside the youth culture competes weakly with peer information and emulation within it.

Effectiveness of current measures

But these currently acceptable (if not politically enacted) measures deserve challenge. Do they even approach the centre of the problem? I think not, for these reasons. First, it seems to be the case that the person who depends is more important in the aetiology of these problems than the substance which may cement and encourage their dependence.

We know that they do not have any characteristic personality features; it also seems to be the case that they have suffered some deep hurt often in early childhood, which is actual or to them apparent rejection. Most substance abusers have no sense of self-worth, nor purpose in life (save to acquire their drug).

Is it not then a paradox that society tries to abate the problem by using social exclusions (expulsion, imprisonment, treatment centres) which can only enhance rejection, alienation, rebellion and low self-worth? After all, if someone has learned that they have no value, there is nothing left in life to strive for, unless it be surrogate satisfactions. Further, if a stable two-parented upbringing in a caring and purposeful family reduces the risks of such rejection and alienation[32] how can we expect these problems to abate in a culture where one third to one half of homes disrupt, children are often ill cared for and job security has fallen abruptly?

The predominant atmosphere in today's society is out of insecurity and mobility, of continual uprooting so that communities can no longer be built or maintained. The very concepts of 'redundancy' and 'unemployment' imply to most who suffer it some kind of social rejection. Should we be surprised if, in this environment, respect for property and for persons is lost whether for others or for self? When someone learns that their value to others is nil save as an industrial transient or 'tool', are they likely to want to behave constructively within society?

If this is the price we must pay for affluence, we should not forget that affluence also increases the availability of the very drugs that dependence looks to abuse. True prevention does not educate or counsel while fostering those influences which enhance the problems. One does not paint the house while it is raining, however good may be the paint or the brushing.

The Christian view

Jesus Christ made the central principles quite clear. In briefest summary they are these; persons have immense worth as creatures of God who can relate to him; a man's life does not consist in what he possesses; the security of love and of relational stability are essential to human well-being.[33,34,35]

Young people today are resentful of a society seen as hypocritical, a society which encourages alcohol, tobacco and gambling while criminalising cannabis and heroin, a society which preaches social responsibility at them while denying basic human needs in its avaricious pursuit of material possessions, its enthronement of money and of power above humanity. It is no surprise that increasing numbers are saying, 'Why should I bother?' These are the kind of considerations that moved Thomas Barnardo 130 years ago.[36]

The way forward

The zeitgeist is now one of autonomy, not paternalism. It is only when a sense of interdependence is recreated that true wealth creation can occur, self respect can return and the desire to pivot self upon gratification can be displaced by the expulsive power of a higher affection.

None of this suggests, or should suggest, that legalising drug substances would remove the problem. Those who support such means should discuss them with people who see the scale of these problems in countries where there are no restrictions, or where those which exist are ineffectual; for example, those concerned with cannabis abuse in Egypt or Pakistan.

My suggestion is rather that to understand and to grapple with these problems we should look deeper than to those levels which are acceptable socially in Britain today. It seems that containment or correction of problems in the existing social structures, though not without some benefits, is unimpressive in its efficacy; only a different kind of coherent social thinking and structure seems likely to do better, a social action which sets personal values above the short-term creation of even greater material wealth.

Notes

1. Cockett R. *Drug Abuse and Personality in Young Offenders.* London: Butterworth, 1971.
2. Nicholi A. The crisis of family disintegration. In: *The Christian Physician and Contemporary Crises.* Report of the Fourth International Congress of Christian Physicians. Toronto: Christian Medical Society of Canada, 1972. p 85.
3. Jasinski DR, Henningfield JE. Conceptual basis of replacement therapies for chemical dependence. In: *Progress in Clinical and Biological Research, 261, Nicotine Replacement: A Critical Evaluation.* (Pomerleau OF, Pomerleau CS eds) New York: Alan R Liss Inc, 1988. pp 13–34.
4. De Alarcon R, Rathod NH. Prevalence and early detection of heroin abuse. BMJ 1968; 2: 549–553.
5. Owens J. Centres for the treatment of drug addiction – integrated approach. BMJ 1967; 1: 501–2.
6. Scottish Home and Health Department. *Understanding Alcohol and Alcoholism in Scotland.* Edinburgh: Scottish Health Education Unit, 1975.
7. Paton WDM. World Medicine, May 22nd, 1974
8. Blum F. *Naloxone and Ethanol Poisoning.* New York: Alan R Liss Inc, 1982.
9. Holman B. Symposium on mechanisms of addiction. Meeting of the British Pharmacological Society, King's College, London, 1988.
10. Caruana S, Scowen P. *Effects of Alcohol on Family Life.*

Alcohol and Alcoholism. Health Visitors' Handbook No. 1. London: Edsall Coy, 1973.

11. Commissioner of Metropolitan Police, Report of a speech to a congress of Life Education International. London: The Times 1994; Sept 23td.

12. Chief Medical Officer's Report. London: HMSO, 1994.

13. Social Trends. London: HMSO, 1994. pp 100–101.

14. Hollister LE. Treatment of drug dependence. Medico-graphia 1981; 4: 23–27.

15. Fraser AC, Cavanagh S. Pregnancy and drug addiction – long-term consequences. J R Soc Med 1991; 84: 530–2.

16. Peto R. *Report on Smoking.* London: Imperial Cancer Research Fund, World Health Organisation and the American College of Surgeons, 1994.

17. Health and Personal Social Services. Statistics for England (1992) London: HMSO, 1993. pp 120–121.

18. Social Trends. London: HMSO, 1977. p 146.

19. Social Trends. London: HMSO, 1992. pp 130–131

20. Barrett GM. The physical ill-effects of alcohol. Update 1981; July: 198–205.

21. Plant MA. The epidemiology of alcohol and illicit drug use. Medicine International 1989; 62: 2538–2542

22. Saunders JB. Alcoholic liver disease. Hospital Update 1982; July: 905–914.

23. Social Trends. London. HMSO, 1982. pp 126–127.

24. Social Trends. London. HMSO, 1993. pp 102–105.

25. Royal College of Physicians. Memorandum on matters relating to the treatment and rehabilitation of drug takers and the prevention of drug misuse, to the Social Services Committee of the House of Commons. London: Royal College of Physicians, 1976.

26. Advisory Committee on Alcoholism: *Report on prevention.* London: HMSO, 1977.

27. Commissioner of Metropolitan Police. Report of a

speech to a congress of Life Education International. London: The Times 1994; Sept 23rd.

28. Kleiner K. Nicotine research 'suppressed' by tobacco company. New Scientist 1994; April 9th: 8–9.

29. Article, reports and letters on tobacco advertising. London: Independent 1994; February 8th, 10th, 11th.

30. Wright JD, Pearl L. Knowledge and experience of young people of drug abuse, 1969–1984. BMJ 1986; 1: 179–182.

31. Methadone shunned in addiction capital. London: The Times 1992; November 16th.

32. White M. Child victims. London: The Times 1994; September 23rd.

33. Luke 6.

34. Matthew 6.

35. Luke 12:15.

36. Vere DW. *Drug Dependence – A New Poverty*. The first Thomas Barnardo Lecture. London: Christian Medical Fellowship, 1971.

CHAPTER FOURTEEN

PROTECTING OUR ENVIRONMENT

R.J. Berry

Professor Berry, an ecological geneticist, is Professor of Genetics at University College London and a former President of the Linnean Society, the British Ecological Society, the European Ecological Federation and Christians in Science. He has written extensively on all aspects of genetics and the environment and was awarded the Templeton UK Individual Award for progress in religion in 1996 for his 'Sustained advocacy of the Christian faith in the world of science'. He gave the Gifford lectures in the University of Glasgow in 1997–8 on 'God, genes, greens and everything'.

Ever since the Age of Enlightenment, we have had an almost boundless faith in our own intelligence and in the benign consequences of our actions. Whatever the discoveries of science, whatever the rate at which we multiplied as a species, whatever the rate at which we destroyed other species, whatever the changes we made to our seas and landscape, we have believed that the world would stay much the same in all its fundamentals. We now know that this is no longer true. This perception could have consequences for national action and international diplomacy as far-reaching as those which resulted from the splitting of the atom . . . We may not be seeing the end of Nature. But Nature is certainly under threat.[1]

> *White Paper on the Environment,*
> This Common Inheritance, *Cm 1200, 1990*

Government strategy documents do not usually base themselves on statements of moral principle, yet the Environment White Paper of 1990 asserted:

> The starting point for this Government is the ethical imperative of stewardship which must underlie all environmental policies. Mankind has always been capable of great good and great evil. This is certainly true of our role as custodians of our planet. The Government's approach begins with the recognition that it is mankind's duty to look after our world prudently and conscientiously . . . We have a moral duty to look after our planet and to hand it on in good order to future generations.[1]

This attitude has been explicitly reaffirmed in the strategy paper on *Sustainable Development*,[2] in which the Government's responses to commitments made at the Rio Summit of 1992 (the United Nations Conference on Environment and Development) are spelt out in detail.

Policy on the environment

Politicians use moral language as part of their normal repartee, but it is highly unusual for official pronouncements to stray beyond specific commitments to action (or inaction). Is there anything that distinguishes policy on the environment from that on say, health, housing or education? The proper answer is that nothing should distinguish it: honourable government should be trustworthy and responsible at all levels and on all subjects. The *reason* why the environment has emerged as a moral issue is that the complexity of environmental pathways means that the consequences of human actions may be far removed in time and space from their causes. When this strikes home, the cumulative reaction can be distressing and compelling. It is not intuitively obvious and therefore all the more shaming that pollution from my local power station may be killing fish and trees hundreds of miles away, or that my fridge or air conditioning is destroying the ozone layer tens of miles above the earth and causing cancers in another continent. Consequently, many of the environmental actions which are needed are essentially altruistic in that they do not help me (or my constituents) at all. Indeed they may actually cause me inconvenience or cost, and help people I have never met and with whom I have no obvious connection. But even though politicians tend to avoid penalising their own constituents—they scream loudly when others damage our environment, such as over-fishing our seas or polluting our pastures with radioactive fall-out—they are forced into action by public outcry when supported by rational persuasion, helped a little by moral courage.[3]

The reality is that political boundaries at all levels (local, regional, national) are irrelevant to many important environmental pathways. We can damage our environment either by sophisticated assaults on it (ironically, often by insulating ourselves from our natural surroundings) or by the sheer pressure of human numbers requiring basic resources such as firewood. And our awareness of such damage is both recent and patchy.

Early environmental concerns

In Britain we have had hunting laws from the beginnings of national legislation. Some of this was to protect the privileges of landowners, although others were concerned with the animals themselves: as early as 1533 Parliament passed an Act declaring a close season for wildfowling. However, the General Inclosure Act of 1845 is generally regarded as the beginning of modern conservation legislation, formally recognising that enclosure was the concern of all local inhabitants and not only the lord and the commoners (i.e.

those who had grazing, fishing or fuel cutting rights). It laid down that the health, comfort and convenience of local people should be taken into account before any enclosure was sanctioned.

The 1845 Act was followed by the setting up in 1865 of the Commons, Open Spaces and Footpaths Preservation Society, formed to resist attempts to enclose common lands around London for building purposes. It is our oldest amenity society and was an important landmark in forming conservation attitudes.

The activities of the Commons Society led in 1893 to the establishment of the National Trust as a land company to buy and accept gifts of land, buildings and common rights for the benefit of the nation. By 1912 the National Trust owned thirteen sites of special interest to naturalists, including Wicken Fen in Cambridgeshire and Cothill in Berkshire.

However, the random way in which potential nature reserves were acquired stimulated Charles Rothschild (second son of the first Lord Rothschild) and his associates to set up a new body, the Society for the Promotion of Nature Reserves (SPNR) 'to preserve for posterity as a national possession some part of our native land, its fauna, flora and geological features'. In fact a main aim was to persuade the National Trust and others to create nature reserves. An early achievement of the SPNR was a schedule of areas of the United Kingdom considered worthy of preservation. This listed the 284 most important potential reserves, with their special characteristics noted. It was submitted to the Board of Agriculture in 1915, and is remarkably similar to that in the Government White Papers of 1947 and 1949, which argued the case for a statutory Nature Conservancy.

Meanwhile the Society for the Prevention of Cruelty to Animals (later the RSPCA) had been founded in 1824 to campaign against cruelty to domesticated animals. This was followed in 1885 by the Selborne Society for the Protection of Birds, Plants and Pleasant Places (later the RSPB), originally a women's organisation concerned to stop thousands of egrets, herons and birds of paradise being slaughtered every year solely for their plumes. These bodies promoted legislation and encouraged public participation in nature protection during the first decades of the present century, but progress was slow, despite successes such as statutory protection for grey seals and a range of bird species.

The next initiative came from the recognition of wasted resources, both material and human. In 1931 E.M. Nicholson and G. Barry stimulated the formation of a non-party research organisation, Political and Economic Planning, which undertook a series of studies of the more pressing economic and social problems of the 1930s. One of the most urgent of these was the decline of heavy industries based around the coalfields, and the concentration of new industries in areas remote from traditional sites, facilitated by the increasing availability of electricity and motor transport. This led to a Royal Commission on the Distribution of the Industrial Population (1937–40), which recommended the setting up of a central planning board.

Following representations from SPNR and RSPB, the Government appointed a committee under Mr Justice Scott to assess the impact this would have on the well-being and preservation of rural communities. The Scott Report (1942) sired yet another committee, on National Parks under Sir Arnold Hobhouse, and this spawned a Wild Life Conservation Special Committee chaired by Julian Huxley. The conclusions of this last committee[4] were instrumental in persuading the Government to set up the Nature Conservancy in 1949 as a Research Council alongside the Science, Medical and Agricultural Councils.

The post-war years

The 1950s and 1960s saw a continuing increase in environmental awareness and education, shown by the growth of such bodies as the RSPB; the development of publishing for naturalists; a massive expansion of adult knowledge, particularly as television became widespread and organisations like the Field Studies Council got into their stride; and the science of ecology entered undergraduate and research programmes.

This phase reached its peak in the early 1970s, particularly with the *Countryside in 1970* conferences under the stimulus of the Duke of Edinburgh, involving the leaders of nearly all the national environmental groups, representatives of farming and landowning interests, and key industrialists and government officials. A major concern at the time was the industrialisation of agriculture and the increasing use of the countryside; measures to conserve wildlife populations could no longer be confined to nature reserves.

The conferences raised consciousness of environmental problems to a new level. During the same period Rachel Carson drew attention[5] to the insidious dangers of persistent pesticides. It is worth recording that British research was at least as advanced, as Norman Moore[6] has expounded elegantly; Monks Wood Experimental Station was opened in 1961 with a remit in part to investigate the ecological effects of pesticides. In 1967 the wreck of the Liberian oil tanker Torrey Canyon off Land's End alerted the British public in a vivid way to the ever-present risks of oil pollution.

The Church of England made its contribution with a General Synod debate on a Working Party report *Man in His Living Environment* which declared that: 'Despoiling the earth is a blasphemy and not just an error of judgement . . . The situation which is created by man's abuse of his power is not God's intention. The deadly sins of avarice, greed, pride destroy the earth. Dust bowls, deserts and a poisoned environment are the consequences.'[7]

In 1972 a computer simulation carried out at Massachusetts Institute of Technology was published under the title *The Limits to Growth*. Its message was that the economic and industrial systems of affluent countries would collapse around the year 2100 unless two correctives were taken: that birth rate should equal death rate, and that capital investment should equal capital depreciation. If these conditions were met, a 'stabilized world model' could result. The authors have recently rerun their model with additional data, and confirmed their earlier prediction,[8] with the ominous addition that, if no constraints are applied, there will be an overshoot in resource misuse, which would exacerbate the subsequent collapse.

The MIT model was taken as the basis for a *Blueprint for Survival*, issued in the *Ecologist* magazine in 1972, and endorsed by a group of leading ecologists. Its argument was that the non-renewable resources which provide the raw materials or energy generation for much of industry are threatened with drastic depletion within a time-span that ordinarily commands politicians' attention, as a result of exponential increase in consumption and of population growth. Moreover, the waste which accompanies this exploitation threatens the processes which sustain human life. The authors of the *Blueprint* proposed a radical reordering of priorities, with industrial societies converting themselves into stable communities characterized by minimum disruption of ecological processes, maximum conservation of materials and energy, and static populations. *The Times* headed its first leader on 14 January 1972, 'The Prophets May Be Right'.

But the calculations of the *Limits to Growth* and the *Blueprint* were rendered void within a few years by the Arab-Israeli wars and the massive increase in the price of fossil fuels. Lord Ashby (who had been the first Chairman of the Royal Commission on Environmental Pollution, set up in 1970) took *A Second Look at Doom* in a lecture at Southampton University in 1975, speaking of the ominous instability of man-made ecosystems. He pointed out that: 'If we experience a shift in the balance of economic power between nations which own resources and nations which need those resources to keep their economies going, one sure consequence would be an increase in tension in the social systems on both sides . . . The tempting way to resolve these tensions is by autocracy and force.'[9] In other words, the period of good-mannered agreement over the use of resources was probably over. Conservation was on the international agenda, but it would be nothing more than a desirable dream unless there was a change of attitudes as well as intellectual assent to impending problems.

1980 onwards

The consensus of the 1970s was destroyed by the disappearance of the myth of cheap energy and the realisation that the issues at stake were too fundamental to be dealt with merely by acknowledging that justice was needed in the use of scarce resources. But the problems agonised over in the *Countryside in 1970* process were (and are) still with us, and in 1980 a *World Conservation Strategy* was produced by the International Union for the Conservation of Nature, the World Wildlife Fund (now the Worldwide Fund for Nature) and the United Nations Environmental Programme.[10] It was an unashamedly utilitarian document, stressing that every aspect of human activity benefits from conservation (and conversely, is as likely to be hindered by environmental mismanagement), and therefore that we have a vested interest to look after our environment. Implicit in it was the concept of 'sustainable development', a theme taken up and expanded in *Our Common Future*, the Report of the World Commission on Environment and Development.[11]

World Conservation Strategy (WCS)

The stated aim of the WCS was to:

(a) maintain essential ecological processes and life-support systems;

(b) preserve genetic diversity;

(c) ensure the sustainable utilisation of species and eco-systems.

The achievement of this aim was assumed to be inevitable, once the problem and possible solutions were defined. This was a major fallacy; right decisions do not automatically spring from accurate knowledge. This is vividly illustrated by the history of clean air legislation. The association between air pollution and death rates was established by John Graunt as early as the mid-seventeenth century. During the nineteenth century there were repeated attempts to pass clean air laws in the UK Parliament, but it was not until the London smog of 1952 led to the abandonment of *La Traviata* at Sadlers Wells and the collapse of prize cattle at the Smithfield Show that comprehensive smoke control legislation was passed. (An excellent account of the political equivocation on this issue is given by Eric Ashby and Mary Anderson.)[12]

The Strategy,[10] being in part a UN document, required responses from member nations of UNEP. The UK response was composed of reports from seven groups, dealing with industry, city, countryside, marine and coastal issues, international policy, education and ethics. The originality in this exercise was the setting up of a group on ethics.[13] Ethics is only mentioned once in the WCS, without elaboration or justification: 'A new ethic, embracing plants and animals as well as people, is required for human societies to live in harmony with the natural world on which they depend for survival and well-being.' This indifference was criticised at a conference held in Ottawa in 1986 to review progress in implementing the Strategy, and it was resolved to include ethics in any revision of the Strategy. The updated Strategy does indeed take on board this recommendation.[14]

The task of the UK ethics group was to put forward

practical proposals about the shaping of sensible attitudes towards the environment in the multidisciplinary no-man's-land where philosophy, psychology, politics, biology and economics meet. The group dealing with education called its report *Education for Commitment*, but something more was needed. I was commissioned to produce the Ethics Report, guided by a Review Group chaired by Lord Ashby and appointed by a national co-ordinating committee.

The Review Group met only once. It was split, apparently irrevocably, between managers and those who regarded our environmental plight as wholly the fault of human incompetence and arrogance. At the time it seemed pointless to pursue this debate. I developed an aphorism that 'we are both a part of nature and apart from nature'. This formed part of our Report which was written by me with considerable help from Lord Ashby and individual discussion with other members of the Group. It would be good to think that this aphorism (or rather, the truth on which it is based) helped to defuse the polarisation in environmental attitudes, at least in the UK where environmental debates have been much more rational and non-confrontational than in some countries. The realisation that sensible environmental actions do not need full agreement on the underlying premises is now gaining ground, but such pragmatic co-operation will always be fragile and liable to failure through challenge of its determining motives.

The Ethics Section of the UK Response to the WCS began with an examination of the factors that determine attitudes, which is where the need for ethics came in; not as a branch of academic philosophy, but in the fundamental sense as an expression of moral understanding 'usually in the form of guide-lines or rules of conduct, involving evaluations of value or worth'.

Environmental value

Value was a key concept, but determining value in the environmental sense is confusing, as at least four different criteria can be applied:

(a) cost in the market-place, quantified as money;
(b) usefulness for individuals or society;
(c) intrinsic worth, which depends on the objective quality of the object valued, in contrast to the market-place cost (which is quantifiable only in relation to the price of other things that can be acquired in its place);
(d) symbolic or conceptual, such as a national flag or liberty.

These four meanings can change independently for the same object. For example, water in a river in highland Scotland or lowland England will be valued differently by an economist since its usefulness will depend on if it:

(a) is drunk, fished or treated as an amenity;
(b) is an object of beauty or a stinking sewer;
(c) acts as a boundary between countries;
(d) forms a barrier to pest spread.

Now, our interest in and therefore valuation of the environment includes self, community and future generations, but nature itself also has its own interest in survival and health. The first three of these interests are clearly anthropocentric; they are the basis of the 1980 WCS. Although they may conflict with each other, in principle some accommodation is usually possible. Considerable advance has been made in recent years by economists recognising that proper accounting involves taking note of both non-material and transgenerational values.

Nature's intrinsic worth

Nature's intrinsic worth is more difficult to justify. The commonest rationalisation is explicitly utilitarian: that we should preserve as many species as possible in case they are useful to us humans (e.g. as a source of anticancer drugs, or the elusive elixir of eternal youth). Ashby[15] has argued that we should learn to value a landscape or biological mechanism in the same way that we are prepared to protect and pay for human artefacts like buildings or paintings. Bryan Norton,[16] an American philosopher, has developed a 'weakly anthropocentric' approach, based on the proposition that we are continually being transformed by our contact with the world around us, which is therefore an integral part of our human development.

The difficulty about defining the intrinsic worth of nature led the Church of England to produce *Our Responsibility for the Living Environment*,[17] a follow-on to its 1969 Report. This was originally intended as a theological reflection on the ethics in the UK Response to the WCS, although its final form was rather wider. Its core was that we live in a world created, redeemed and sustained by God; since this is God's world, not ours, it has intrinsic worth. Interestingly (and encouragingly) the implication (although perhaps not the theology) of this point was taken up in the Government White Paper on the environment, *This Common Inheritance*. Citing Mrs Thatcher (who in turn, drew upon John Ruskin), the White Paper affirmed, 'We do not hold a freehold on our world, but only a full repairing lease. We have a moral duty to look after our planet and to hand it on in good order to future generations.' John Major used very similar words in his speech to the Earth Summit in Rio.

Perceived failures

The idea that we are running out of world is commonly expressed as a vague but compelling worry that 'something is wrong'; that science has failed to deal fairly and adequately with human needs,[18,19] while religion is perceived as either too personal or too remote to cope with the real complexities of twentieth-century life.

What is the way forward? We can agree there is a problem, but there is certainly no generally accepted solution. There is a common belief that the Judaeo-Christian tradition from which Western science and technology sprang has been one of the main problems because

> If one seeks licence for those who would increase radio-activity, create canals and harbours with atomic bombs, employ poisons without constraint, or give consent to the bulldozer mentality, there could be no better injunction than the text 'God blessed them (the newly formed human beings) and said to them, Be fruitful and increase, fill the earth and subdue it, have dominion over the fish in the sea, the birds of the air, and everything that moves on the earth' (Genesis 1:28) . . . Dominion and subjugation must be expunged as the biblical injunction of man's relation to nature.[20]

And 'the first step must be plainly to reject and to scrub out the complacent image of Man the Conqueror of Nature, and of Man Licensed by God to conduct himself as the earth's worst pest.'[21]

The most frequently quoted indictment of Christianity is that of an American historian Lynn White, who declared in a lecture to the American Association for the Advancement of Science that 'Christianity . . . insisted that it is God's will that man exploit nature for his proper ends . . . Christianity bears a huge burden of guilt.'[22] White's thesis was based on the premise that our increasing ability to control and harness natural forces was flawed by the assumption that, 'We are superior to nature, contemptuous of it, willing to use it for our slightest whim . . . We shall continue to have a worsening ecological crisis until we reject the Christian axiom that nature has no reason for existence but to serve man . . . Both our present science and our present technology are so tinctured with orthodox Christian arrogance towards nature that no solution for our ecological crisis can be expected from them alone.' But, and this is a key inference, 'Since the roots of our trouble are so largely religious, the remedy must be essentially religious, whether we call it that or not.' White went on to conclude that our main hope should be a refocused Christianity, not a wholesale repudiation of it. He suggested that we should return to the 'alternative Christian view of nature and man's relation to it', exemplified by Francis of Assisi's respect for the living world. He proposed Francis as a patron saint for ecologists; in 1980 Pope John Paul II accepted the idea.

However the malignant effects of Judaeo-Christianity can be overstressed. Running parallel to the 'dominance' tradition is an equally strong stewardship theme.[23] Indeed, stewardship has been the key to the Christian attitude to nature for most of the Church's history. It was implicit in the Celtic Church of the Dark Ages and is explicit in the Benedictine Rule which was a major influence shaping society in the Middle Ages. It is a doctrinal corrective to unfettered human dominance on two grounds:

(a) God's command in Genesis was in the context of human beings created in his image', which involves trust-worthiness and responsibility.
(b) Hebrew kingship was meant to be a servant-kingship, exemplified by the instructions given to David and Solomon, and ideally shown by Jesus Christ; it was not a despotic potency.

Solomon, and ideally shown by Jesus Christ; it was not a despotic potency.

This is not to deny that the attitudes condemned by McHarg[20] and Nicholson[21] have been uncommon. To some extent they can be attributed to rationalisation by farmers of their increasing success over 'nature' as technology developed. But the fact that a biblical text was frequently misinterpreted should not be allowed to usurp its correct interpretation.

Despite the habit of blaming Christianity for our environmental disasters, a quick survey shows that environmental degradation is almost universal whenever excessive strain is put on natural systems. Leaving aside the horrors produced in Eastern Europe under specifically anti-religious regimes, in other places overgrazing, deforestation and the like on a scale sufficient to destroy civilisations has been committed by Egyptians, Assyrians, Romans, North Africans, Persians, Indians, Aztecs and Buddhists. Japan has pollution problems as bad as anywhere in the world. Jacques Delors has commented, 'I have to say that the Oriental religions have failed to prevent to any marked degree the appropriation of the natural environment . . . Despite different traditions, the right to use or exploit nature seems to have found in industrial countries the same economic justification.'

Ecoreligion

Perhaps in response to all these failures, there has been a trend in recent years to develop various forms of ecoreligion, sometimes based on established faiths, but more often on an eccentric rag-bag of beliefs. The problems of uncontrolled eclecticism is illustrated by the fate of the 'Assisi Declarations' produced by some of the major world faiths (Buddhism, Christianity, Hinduism, Islam, Judaism and Baha'i) at the twenty-fifth anniversary celebration of the

Worldwide Fund for Nature in 1986. These innocuous and laudable statements led to the establishment of an international 'Network of Conservation and Religion', a useful initiative. But attempts to further the aims of bringing together conservation and religion have led to some highly contentious activities, such as some Cathedral Creation Celebrations involving wholly incompatible philosophies, with joint worship by people of different religions improperly joining different faiths, including monotheists and polytheists. For example, the Coventry celebration in 1988 included a prayer, 'Our brothers and sisters of the creation, the mighty trees, the broad oceans, the air, the earth, the creatures of creation, forgive us and reconcile us to you.'

Such heterodoxy stimulated in 1991 an 'open letter' signed by over 2,000 Church of England clergy, and stating:

> We desire to love and respect people of other faiths. We respect their rights and freedoms. We wholeheartedly support co-operation in appropriate community, social, moral and political issues between Christians and those of other faiths wherever this is possible . . . [but] We are deeply concerned about gatherings for interfaith worship and prayer involving Christian people . . . We believe these events, however motivated, conflict with the Christian duty to proclaim the gospel. They imply that salvation is offered by God not only through Jesus Christ but by other means and thus deny his uniqueness and finality as the only Saviour.

New Age movement

More insidious and difficult to confront are the beliefs underlying the so-called New Age movement. 'New Age' has no precise meaning, but it is claimed to be a sign of the time when the world is moving from Pisces dominated by Christianity, to Aquarius symbolising unity. Such a faith (if that is an appropriate description) is necessarily pantheistic and relativistic (since there are no right/wrong distinctions);

salvation is achieved through self-realisation, so various human potential movements are claimed by New-Agers.

The present manifestation of the New Age derives from sundry utopianisms of the eighteenth and nineteenth centuries (especially the Theosophical Society), but it has its immediate roots in the anti-authoritarianism of the 1960s, with its appeals to romanticism as an antidote to the presumed determinism of science. Whereas mainstream thought accepted the need for environmental management and statutory controls, the emerging green movement sought the removal of constraints, allowing life to be lived in harmony with the earth. Key concepts were balance, stability and peace. A seminal document was E.F. Schumacher's *Small is beautiful*[24] with its emphasis on appropriate or intermediate technology. Big business and central government are distrusted. Tradition and authority are suspect, but selectively endorsed in the guise of earth myths and native customs. Green religion tends to be a passionate animism.

Some of this is healthy. It is right to examine traditions, test authority, and seek to improve the structures of society. But it is too easy to jettison truth in the course of rethinking, while the situation is complicated by the vast spectrum of beliefs and practices between the extreme Greens and the most orthodox establishmentarians.

The environmental complaint

Neither science nor religion by themselves can produce the answer to our environmental problems. The toothlessness of science alone was recognized by the lack of impact of the World Conservation Strategy, which fell into the Enlightenment fallacy that knowledge automatically produces response. It was underlined by the calling forth of the Assisi Declarations by the Worldwide Fund for Nature and its support for a conservation and religion network. It was made explicit by the Duke of Edinburgh when setting up a consultation on *Christianity and the Environment*[25] posing the question, 'There must be a moral as well as a practical argument for environmental conservation. What is it?' The confusions of religion are illustrated by uncertainties about whether to preserve or manage, about the role of established faiths or traditions, by the selective misuse of scientific data.

Karl Popper has written: 'The fact that science cannot make any pronouncement about ethical principles has been misinterpreted as indicating that there are no such principles, while in fact the search for truth presupposes ethics.' Is it possible to produce a generally acceptable environmental ethic? The answer to this must be yes.

In 1989, the Economic Summit Nations (the G7) called a conference in Brussels on *Environmental ethics*. In the words of its final communiqué, the participants 'benefited from a high degree of convergence between people of different cultures, East and West, and a wide variety of disciplines'. There was absolute unanimity among those present that the main need for individuals and nations alike was to practice responsible stewardship. On behalf of the conference, I chaired a Working Party over the succeeding year to formulate a *Code of Environmental Practice*.[26]

The Code went to the G7 Heads of State meeting in Texas in 1990. It is based on a simple ethic: *stewardship of the living and non-living systems of the earth in order to maintain their sustainability for present and future, allowing development with forbearance and fairness*. In itself, this is an innocuous statement, indeed almost vacuous. However, it entails characteristics common to all good citizens, as well as states and corporations, involving responsibility, freedom, justice, truthfulness, sensitivity, awareness and integrity. In turn these lead to a series of obligations which are its teeth and may involve real cost.

The Code is a secular document, produced by a secular group for a secular organisation. It was one of the documents submitted as a source paper for the 'Earth Charter' which was intended to preface the work of the UN Conference on Environment and Development in Rio (but which succumbed to political expediency, and was replaced by an anodyne 'Rio Declaration').[27] But it was taken almost in its entirety by a Working Party of the General Synod of the Church of England charged with preparing 'a statement of Christian stewardship in relation to the whole of creation to challenge government, Church and people'.[28]

Christian stewardship

The General Synod paper began with a statement of Christian understanding:

> We all share and depend on the same world, with its finite and often non-renewable resources. Christians believe that this world belongs to God by creation, redemption and sustenance, and that he has entrusted it to humankind, made in his image and responsible to him; we are in the position of stewards, tenants, curators, trustees or guardians, whether or not we acknowledge this responsibility.
>
> Stewardship implies caring management, not selfish exploitation; it involves a concern for both present and future as well as self, and a recognition that the world we manage has an interest in its own survival and well-being independent of its value to us.[28]

It then drew out the implications of such stewardship in the same way (and in almost the same language) as the Brussels Code. Christian doctrine provides an additional theoretical underpinning for the secular conclusions, but the practical outworking of both sacred and secular is identical-as indeed Christians ought to expect, since they believe God created, ordained and sustains the world for righteous and unrighteous alike. Orthodox Christian doctrine is that God is both transcendent and immanent: outside and controlling the world, and inside and influencing it (as anyone who prays in faith accepts).

Jonathan Porritt has claimed that the Christian error is to believe in a God far away and remote, whereas the discovery of Green religionists is that God is within and intimate. Porritt's version demonstrates only too clearly the Church's failure to claim and expound sound doctrine, as well as the Greens' acceptance of a half-truth as potentially distorting as was the opposite half-truth, exemplified two centuries ago by Paley's 'Divine Watchmaker'.

The separation of God and creation is important. The clear teaching of the Bible is that the link between creator and created is the Word of God; creation is not divine, it is not God, and it is related to God through us ('made in God's image'). The problem ought not to be walking a tightrope between immanence and transcendence, but an unapologetic trinitarianism. The world is redeemed from being merely an object by Christ's work, and is upheld and ordered by the Spirit. If we see the way forward as a balance between a distant God of absolute power and a confusing pan(en)theism, we will find ourselves repeatedly having to readjust the balance. If, on the other hand, we follow Irenaeus and Tertullian in insisting on a God who alone is self-existent and who created out of nothing, we avoid the dangers of both dualism and a self-centred religion knowable only through self-realisation. The contemporary New Age debate is really a rerun of the gnostic debate of the early centuries AD.

All this means that there is more to a Christian understanding of the environment than calculating stewardship. If we are not careful, stewardship becomes just one more command to obey; indeed in the industrial world, environmental care is commonly reduced to conformity in meeting statutory requirements, rather than an attitude of respect and moral responsibility. Chris Patten, when Secretary of

State for the Environment, described the ideal well (in a lecture given at Godolphin & Latymer School in 1990):

> The relationship between man and his environment depends, and always will depend, on more than just sound science and sound economics. For individuals part of the relationship is metaphysical. Those of us with religious convictions can, if we are lucky, experience the beauties as well as the utilities of the world as direct manifestations of the love and creative power of God.

Conclusions

A major part of the 'metaphysical relationship' extolled by Patten is experiential. It was awe and wonder which led such different characters as John Muir, Julian Huxley and Teilhard de Chardin to seek a rationalisation for their experiences. It is more than a quest or challenge, or a desire for like companionship that produces escape to the wilds. But I would urge there is something deeper, towards which wilderness-seekers are groping. Whether the symptoms are middle-class involvement in recycling, countryside protection or ecoconsumerism, or more radical New Age commitments to self-discovery, there is a widespread recognition of a missing 'order' in modern society. In primitive societies, the constant battle to survive means this 'disorder' is submerged. This may be the reason for 'return to nature' cults; other people's grass is always greener than one's own, and native societies are commonly perceived to have a wisdom and peace that has disappeared from more advanced cultures. But this is an illusion, well illustrated by Thor Heyerdahl, who wrote after a year on an 'unspoilt' Pacific island in the Marquesa group where he and his wife had found disease, distrust and misery:

There is no Paradise to be found on earth today. There are people living in great cities who are far happier than the majority of those in the South Seas. Happiness comes from within, we realise that now. It is in his mind and way of life that man may find his Paradise-the ability to perceive the true values of life, which are far removed from property and riches, or from power and renown.

Robin Grove-White, former Director of the CPRE, has come to the same conclusion: 'Rather than the environmental agenda being presented to us from on high by science, the actual selection of issues . . . arise from human beings responding gropingly to a sense of the ways in which their moral, social and physical identities are being threatened.'[29] Grove-White identifies the way forward as new theological understandings of the human person and its needs. I believe he is right in seeing the key to environmental sense in human nature; Lynn White said much the same twenty-five years ago, 'What we do about nature depends on our ideas of the man—nature relationship.'[22]

But we do not need new understandings; our starting point is the ancient, universally established and often-disguised selfishness and pride of the individual. Our greed is at the root of all environmental damage—sometimes expressed as personal wants, sometimes through corporate action, sometimes as a simple desire to demonstrate power. This is common ground to all major religions.

The distinguishing trait of the Christian faith is that God has taken action to deal with the problem.[30] Christians have a particular responsibility to the environment because of their acknowledgement and worship of God as creator, redeemer and sustainer. For them, abuse of the natural world is disobedience to God, not merely an error of judgement. This means that Christians must examine their life-style and work out their attitudes to the natural world as part of their service and stewardship. It also means affirming a God who is neither remote nor powerless.

The Church of England Doctrine Commission put it thus:

> To accept God as the Creator of all things implies that man's own creative activity should be in co-operation with the purposes of the Creator who has made all things good. To accept man's sinfulness is to recognize the limitation of human goals and the uncertainty of human achievement. To accept God as Saviour is to work out our own salvation in union with him, and so to do our part in restoring and recreating what by our folly and frailty we have defaced or destroyed, and in helping to come to birth those good possibilities of creation that have not yet been realised . . . To hold that God has created the world for a purpose gives man a worthy goal in life and a hope to lift up his heart and to strengthen his efforts. To believe that man's true citizenship is in heaven and that his true identity lies beyond space and time enables him both to be involved in this world and yet to have a measure of detachment from it that permits radical changes such as would be scarcely possible if all his hopes were centred on this world. To believe that all things will be restored and nothing wasted gives added meaning to all man's efforts and strivings. Only by the inspiration of such a vision is society likely to be able to re-order this world and to find the symbols to interpret man's place within it.[31]

The tragedy of modern society—even that part which worships God-is that (in J.B. Phillips' words) its God is too small. The God of twentieth-century Westerners is a God of the gaps, squeezed into the ever-shrinking gaps of knowledge. But the Christian God is Lord of all; he is Lord of creation as well as the Church. God so loved the *cosmos*— not merely the human world—that he sent his only Son to die for it.

But how does theology translate into environmental protection? Does Government have any role, other than maintaining an ordered society where individuals can exercise their freedom to choose and hence provide a stage for the exercise of responsible stewardship? The answer to this question about government is emphatically 'yes', and for at least three reasons:

(a) The long pathways in the environment between action and effect mean that an individual or society may unwittingly damage others distant in space or time. Examples of this are distorted trade patterns penalising primary producers or even more insidiously, depleting non-renewable resources (such as fossil fuels) leading to slow and possibly non-reversible changes for future generations (such as global warming). Responsible government may require actions which are contrary to the immediate interests of the governed (who may be their electors). At the time of writing it is not clear how many nations are going to fulfil the pledges to limit carbon dioxide emissions they made in the Climate Change Convention at Rio (for the problems and possibilities for the United Kingdom, see Holdaway[32]).

(b) A national government may be unwilling to introduce needed legislation (such as pollution control or fishing or lumbering restrictions) because its own subjects will be placed at a disadvantage. This means that international agreements are necessary so that everyone has a 'level playing-field'. The agreements on trade in endangered species (CITES) and on phasing out chloro-fluorohydrocarbons are only forerunners of the many such conventions that will be required in coming years. The environment does not respect national boundaries.

(c) The environmental disasters produced in Eastern Europe under centralised command economies are now distressingly clear. However, and despite the claims of extreme free marketeers,[33] there is no intrinsic reason why market economies should necessarily be good for the environment, for the simple reason that the market forces affecting the environment are not 'perfect' ones, and that the market cannot properly evaluate the range of personal values, never mind those of nature. The 'environmental movement' may be divided, other-worldly, often distracted by *causes celebres*, but it represents a mixture of fear and aspirations which is increasingly forcing politicians and negotiators on environmental matters to seek common ground more than in other sorts of areas,[34] and to provide leadership rather than mere crisis management.

Environmental concern waxes and wanes, but it will never go away for the blindingly obvious reason that there are more and more of us on this finite planet, using (often misusing) a finite pool of resources. We may discover new resources, we may substitute new materials for exhausted ones, but we can never escape the fact that our treatment of the environment will affect the survival of our children's children.

I end as I began, with the UK Government's own expressed action plan as stated in *This Common Inheritance*:

> In order to fulfil its responsibility of stewardship the Government bases its policies and proposals on a number of supporting principles.
>
> 1. We must base our policies on fact not fantasy, and use the best evidence and analysis available;
> 2. Given the environmental risks, we must act responsibly and be prepared to take precautionary action where it is justified;

3. We must inform public debate and public concern by ensuring publication of the facts;
4. We must work for progress just as hard in the international arena as we do at home; and
5. We must take care to choose the best instruments to achieve our environmental goals.

Acknowledgements

This chapter is in part reproduced by permission from a Templeton Lecture delivered to the Royal Society of Arts in London (*RSA Journal* 1993; 141: 305–318) and also as Chapter 12 of Atkinson D., ed, *Pastoral Ethics* (Oxford: Lynx, 1994).

Notes

1. *This Common Inheritance: Britain's Environmental Strategy.* London: HMSO, 1990. Cm 1200, paras 1.8, 1.10, 1.14.
2. *Sustainable Development. The UK Strategy.* London: HMSO, 1994. Cm 2426, para. 1.8.
3. Ashby, E. Foreword. In *Environmental Dilemmas. Ethics and Decisions* (Berry RJ ed). London: Chapman & Hall, 1993. pp xiv-xxii.
4. Wild life Conservation Special Committee. *Conservation of Nature in England and Wales.* London: HMSO, 1947. Cmd 7122.
5. Carson R. *Silent Spring.* Boston: Houghton Mifflin, 1962.
6. Moore NW. *Bird of Time.* Cambridge: Cambridge University Press, 1987.
7. *Man in His Living Environment.* London: Church Assembly, 1969.
8. Meadows DH, Meadows DL, Randers J. *Beyond the*

Limits: Global Collapse or a Sustainable Future. London: Earthscan, 1992.

9. Ashby E. *A Second Look at Doom.* Twenty-first Fawley Foundation Lecture. Southampton: University of Southampton, 1975.

10. *World Conservation Strategy.* Gland, Switzerland: International Union for the Conservation of Nature, United Nations Environmental Programme, World Wildlife Fund, 1980.

11. *Our Common Future.* The Report of the World Commission on Environment and Development ('The Brundtland Report'). Oxford: Oxford University Press, 1987.

12. Ashby E, Anderson M. *The Politics of Clean Air.* Oxford: Clarendon Press, 1981.

13. *Conservation and Development Programme for the UK.* A Response to the World Conservation Strategy. London: Kogan Page, 1983.

14. *Caring for the Earth.* A strategy for sustainable living. Gland, Switzerland: International Union for the Conservation of Nature, United Nations Environmental Programme, World Wide Fund for Nature, 1991.

15. Ashby E. *Reconciling Man with the Environment.* London: Oxford University Press, 1978.

16. Norton BG. *Why Preserve Natural Variety?* Princeton, NJ: Princeton University Press, 1987.

17. *Our Responsibility for the Living Environment.* London: Church Information Office, 1986.

18. Appleyard B. *Understanding the Present: Science and the Soul of Modern Man.* London: Picador, 1992.

19. Midgley M. *Science as Salvation.* London: Routledge, 1992.

20. McHarg IL. *Design with Nature.* New York: Natural History, 1969.

21. Nicholson EM. *The Environmental Revolution.* London: Hodder & Stoughton, 1970.

22. White L. *The Historical Roots of our Ecologic Crisis.* *Science, NY* 1967; 155: 1204–1207.

23. Attfield R. *The Ethics of Environmental Concern.* Oxford: Basil Blackwell, 1983; (Revised edition), Athens, GA: University of Georgia Press, 1991.

24. Schumacher EF, *Small is Beautiful.* London: Blond & Briggs, 1973.

25. Duke of Edinburgh, Mann M. *Survival or Extinction. A Christian Attitude to the Environment.* Windsor: St George's House, 1989.

26. Berry RJ. Environmental Concern. In, *Environmental Dilemmas. Ethics and Decisions* (Berry RJ ed). London: Chapman & Hall, 1993. pp 242–264.

27. Grubb M, Koch M, Munson A, Sullivan F, Thomson K. *The Earth Summit Agreements.* London: Earthscan for the Royal Institute of International Affairs, 1993.

28. *Christians and the Environment.* A Report by the Board for Social Responsibility. London: General Synod Misc. 367, 1991.

29. Grove-White R. Human Identity and the Environment Crisis. In, *The Earth Beneath* (Ball I, Goodall M, Palmer C, Reader J. eds). London: SPCK, 1992. pp 13–34.

30. Colossians 1:16–20.

31. Montefiore H (ed). *Man and Nature.* London: Collins, 1975.

32. Holdaway H. Energy and the Environment. Towards a Sustainable UK Strategy. Proceedings of a consultation held at St George's House, Windsor Castle, 7–9 June 1993. Energy & Environment 1993; 5: 416–450.

33. *Man and Nature.* Irvington-on-Hudson, NY: Foundation for Economic Education, 1993.

34. Brenton T. *The Greening of Machiavelli.* London: Earthscan for the Royal Institute of Environmental Affairs, 1994.

CHAPTER FIFTEEN

A CHRISTIAN LIFE-STYLE

John Taylor

Bishop Taylor was Bishop of St Albans from 1980–95. He was Lord High Almoner to HM the Queen from 1988–1997 and is President of The National Club.

The reader who has got thus far may well be feeling dazed by the complexity and variety of the issues which have been touched upon in earlier chapters. Little attempt has been made to suggest solutions to the enormous problems which have been laid out for the reader's consideration. Indeed, only a fool would offer solutions: the issues are too vast and there are no easy answers. Rather, what the contributors have sought to do has been to show from their own knowledge of their subjects what has been done, what remains to be done and what appears to be insoluble. The book is not a catalogue of achievements but a collection of concerns, each one of major importance for the health and well-being of our Nation.

There are of course omissions. Nothing is said about Third World issues and the intractable problem of national debt and a fairer sharing out of the world's resources—an ethical concern to which every Christian has to give attention. This is not a compendium of morality themes, a handbook of ethical issues. Instead it is a small cross-section of subjects on which The National Club has persuaded its members or friends to contribute, as an indicator of the dilemmas on which we as Christians need to be better informed. The exercise is unashamedly educational, both for ourselves who enjoy membership of the Club and for any who care to read it.

These chapters may at the same time trigger off a sense of hopelessness. What, we wonder, can we do to turn the tide, to see a way through the problems, to influence the course of this great juggernaut called 'society', which will be of any use against the forces of evil or selfishness, materialism or ignorance that appear to be in control? While we may be thankful that better minds than ours are grappling with all these problems, we know they are not infallible and that in any case they are struggling with little hope of any neat solution. So is there anything that we as ordinary Christian people can do? What can the individual do to influence the society in which he or she may live?

A degree of optimism

I would want to answer those questions with a degree of optimism, and that optimism is reflected in this closing chapter. There is much that we can do. We need never despair of our own apparent ineffectiveness. A shepherd-boy with a sling and five stones was able to deal with Goliath,[1] and the history and example of the Christian Church have provided endless examples of the power of the dedicated individual to change the course of history. But I am not concerned with super-heroes or even with heroes in the making. There are the modest unsung heroes whose chief claim to fame is that they have shone as lights in dark places. You find them in offices and factories, in schools and hospitals, on housing estates and in voluntary organisations, in local government and in our churches. They are recognisable because people know that if they were not there, the community would be infinitely the poorer. A very few of them can now be nominated for public recognition through the Honours List. A handful are given a royal token of the community's esteem as the recipients of the Royal Maundy. The vast majority receive no such reward. They are the unseen, unsung saints of the community.

So it can be done. A little leaven can and does leaven the whole lump. The character and personality of one person can make a far wider impact for good than most of us realise. It is on that theme that I want this book to end.

Social disintegration

There is an urgency about all this. We urgently need to rediscover the importance of developing a more Christian life-style in the life of our Nation. There is a real danger of social breakup as more and more emphasis is placed on the individual and the goal of personal self-fulfilment. Morality has been privatised along with religion and the public utilities. As in the days of the Judges[2] everyone does that which is right in his own eyes, and usually rightness is interpreted as what seems appropriate and best for me. In my judgement the two areas of life most at risk are the integrity of the family and the place of authority.

Integrity of the family

The Church of England missed a great opportunity in its recent report on the family, entitled *Something to Celebrate*. The impression was given that the celebration being called for was for the very varied forms of family life that exist today, some of which could hardly be recognised as families in the traditional sense, simply as relationships. The report appeared to be doing little more than baptise the highly unsatisfactory status quo, from single parent units to same-sex relationships. By rejecting the concept of living in sin (an absolute gift to the media) they guaranteed that the report would not be read and that its many good features would sink below the surface. The institution of the family as God's gift for the education and nurture of humanity still needs its advocates and apologists, as well as its icons and exemplars. At present it is known more for its fractures and failures than for its blessings and benefits.

Breakdown of authority

There must be some link, though not necessarily causal, between the present state of the family in Great Britain and the widespread breakdown of authority. It was the former Archbishop of York, Lord Habgood, who articulated the phrase (whether his or someone else's) about 'the culture of contempt' which has been spreading like a cancer through our society. It is damagingly pervasive and its infection is well-nigh irresistible. It attacks not only the institutions of the nation—the monarchy, the Government, the Church, the law—but all sorts of authority figures from parents to teachers, from doctors to social workers. It has not been helped by the vogue for satire in contemporary entertainment and its legacy is the climate of dismissiveness and suspicion which assumes that everyone has something to hide and that therefore no one is believed or taken at face value. Pedestals are only there to be taken down. Respect is at a premium, for no one is really worthy of it.

Backlash

This state of affairs invites a backlash, and from time to time we have seen signs of one. There is always the fear that it may take some neo-fascist form, but the acceptable signs have been the wholesale sense of revulsion that swept through the nation at the time of the murders of Jamie Bulger and more recently of Philip Lawrence. And with the revulsion came the perplexity: how could our civilised, liberal society ever have produced such decadence? The need for a restoration of national morality became a talking point in every newspaper and on every radio and television magazine programme. The thoughtless ones concentrated on pinning blame—on the Government, the Church, our schools, the family. Few tackled it by looking at themselves. What can I do?

Standards in schools

As far as the schools are concerned, an important break-through came in an address given to a London conference in January 1996 by Dr Nick Tate, the chief executive of the School Curriculum and Assessment Authority. He was appealing for a nation-wide debate on values and spiritual education and was suggesting a revised form of educational Ten Commandments for use in schools, covering honesty, punctuality, fair play and self-discipline. The fact that this is to be carried through with the help of a National Forum on Values and Society, which could turn out to be nothing but another quango, should not conceal the more important fact of the wide media coverage given to Dr Tate's speech. This in itself demonstrates that it is something the general public are longing to hear said and are crying out for something to be done about it. We heartily commend Dr Tate and applaud the Christian principles which have prompted the initiative he and his Authority have begun to take.

Personal morality

There is of course much more to this than the class-room, though that is never a bad place to start. Morality stems from values and beliefs and the surest way to ensure the growth of higher moral standards in our nation is through the revival of godliness. It has become almost a cliché to point to the effect on the British nation of the religious awakening associated with the names of John and Charles Wesley, which produced such a new spirit within the community that even secular historians have had grudgingly to acknowledge the fact. Less well-known but equally well documented is the story told in Northern Ireland of the religious revival that swept throughout Ulster through the evangelistic missions of Willie Nicholson in the 1920s. It is said that the moral tone of Belfast's docklands was so raised that the dockyard managers had to erect new stores to house the stolen tools that were returned by Nicholson's converts!

Role of the churches

Without any doubt there is a heavy responsibility laid upon our churches to work and pray towards the goal of religious awakening. We believe that nothing short of this will produce the effect that so many of our nation, religious and irreligious, keenly desire. Through their commitment to the Decade of Evangelism the churches are playing their part in accepting this responsibility and many are watching carefully to see whether or not it is succeeding. Results so far suggest that inroads are being made. Attitudes are slowly changing. Churches are becoming more outward-looking, less geared to survival and more to mission. New people are being brought into the churches, but mainly as adults, and the young are still an untouched mission-field. There is undoubtedly much more that needs to be done. The churches with the least tradition, the new neo-pentecostal churches, are doing best, according to all the surveys, but nowhere is there ground for complacency.

What can be done?

But we come back to the original question: what can I do to stem the tide, to make a difference? And here I want to list the leavening, community-changing characteristics of the Christian life-style which the individual Christian is called upon to embody in his or her life. True, we are called to live out these qualities for the sake of our God and not just because it will do others good. Our calling is to please him and to obey his will. But in so doing we shall be playing our part as good citizens and good neighbours, to the inevitable benefit of those among whom we live and work. The list, I hasten to add, is typical and not complete.

Living a life of transparent integrity

This is more than just honesty, it is nearer to the biblical quality of holiness, though the word conjures up all kinds of misleading images in today's world. It involves openness to God and to one's fellows, having a clear direction in life, holding to the highest standards of truth, being sensitive to the dangers of self-deception, willing to admit mistakes and failures, and in someone's colourful phrase, having the same goods in the shop as are in the windows.

Caring for others, especially those less fortunate than oneself

This is of the essence of Christian love. 'If any one has the world's goods and sees his brother in need, yet closes his heart against him, how does God's love abide in him?'[3] Such charity is a long-standing Christian virtue, but it must not be confined to the collection plate and the countless good causes that jostle for our attention and our donations. It also includes the virtue of hospitality as well as the social concern that determines to do something to eradicate the circumstances that cause many of our social problems. It may well have a political side to it.

Support for authority, not least in prayer

There is an honourable Christian tradition of defiance against those rulers who flagrantly flout God's commands and do despite to their people's freedom, but the norm of Christian behaviour is to pray for and to support those who are set in authority over us. If the apostle Paul was advocating such attitudes towards a pagan Roman emperor and his underlings, we need to be careful not to let our personal disagreements with a particular government or regime undermine what should be a basic loyalty to the powers that be, more especially when they have been placed there by the democratic process. While such loyalty does not rule out criticism (there is nothing unchristian about being a member of Her Majesty's opposition), it does put an embargo on law-breaking and it also accepts whole-heartedly the right of the duly elected government to govern.

Maintaining positive rather than negative attitudes

One of the most eroding influences in the early Church was caused by 'murmuring'. We read about it in the Bible in connection with the payment of widows' benefit[4] and it needed immediate action in the appointment of deacons who could ensure fair play. Elsewhere in the Bible[5] the sin of grumbling is coupled with many of the grosser sins, showing just how seriously undermining of morale it could be—and still is. By contrast the Christian is to be positive, supportive, optimistic even. After all, he has something to be optimistic about, unlike many with no comparable faith. It is the Christian virtue of hope, or hopefulness, which is built upon the belief that God is in control and that righteousness will prevail. An injection of that spirit does wonders for any community and it is all too frequently in short supply.

A sense of accountability

One of the unique features of the Christian religion is that those who embrace it carry within them the knowledge that they will one day be called to account for their behaviour and attitudes. More than that, the Christian is aware of the need to keep short accounts with God and to practise periodic self-examination, leading to confession of sin and where necessary restitution. This does not in any way guarantee freedom from self-delusion (we all have an inbuilt blindness factor) but it does induce an abiding sense of moral responsibility and a proper and healthy susceptibility to the voice of conscience, moulded as it must always be by being regularly steeped in the teachings of Holy Scripture. In my experience there is no better way of developing moral fibre and the courage to be different from the crowd.

A spirit of sacrifice

The wording of the old prayer says it all: 'To fight and not to heed the wounds, to toil and not to seek for rest, to labour and not to ask for any reward save that of knowing that we do thy will.'[6] This is not the quality of being prepared to sacrifice oneself for a given cause, however worthy; it is the dedication of the whole life to God for his service and the welfare of our fellow men and women. It is a sacrificial principle which draws its strength and its example from the sacrificial death of Jesus Christ, the Son of God. For his sake nothing is too much to ask, no sacrifice too great, no demand too costly. The one who died for us and for the forgiveness of our sins and who rose again from the dead to bring us reconciliation with God demands, and rightly so, that degree of allegiance. The Christian therefore is always striving for the highest and finds fulfilment and contentment in doing so.

Here then are some of the features of the Christian life-style which we maintain would do so much to benefit our nation. They cannot be imposed on unwilling victims. They spring out of a revived and renewed commitment to faith in Jesus Christ, which should always be our goal both for ourselves and for others. Everyone who professes that faith is under obligation to live it out and to encourage others to do the same. It will not provide the answer to those massive questions that this little book has been addressing, but it cannot but help. Few would deny that the need is great and that urgency presses.

In the Church of England at the present time, issues of Christian stewardship are understandably to the forefront. Dioceses have resorted to what they call TRIO campaigns, and generally speaking they have been remarkably successful but that is another story. My point is the meaning of the acronym TRIO, because it sums up the message of this chapter and this whole book.

It stands for The Responsibility Is Ours.

Notes

1. 1 Samuel 17.
2. Judges 21:25.
3. 1 John 3:17.
4. Acts 6.
5. Jude 16.
6. St Ignatius of Loyola (1491–1556).